AMERICAN RENEWAL EXTENDED EDITION

A MANIFESTO FOR RESISTANCE, A BLUEPRINT FOR RESTORATION, AND A VISION FOR REDEMPTION NOW WITH READER'S GUIDES

AMERICAN RENEWAL
BOOK 1

JIM VINCENT

American Renewal: Extended Edition

© 2025 Jim Vincent

All rights reserved.

No part of this publication may be reproduced, stored in a retrieval system, or transmitted in any form or by any means—electronic, mechanical, photocopy, recording, or otherwise—without the prior written permission of the publisher, except for brief quotations used in reviews, articles, or scholarly analysis.

This is a work of nonfiction. Every effort has been made to ensure accuracy. Any errors are the responsibility of the author. Opinions expressed are the author's own and do not represent any organization or institution. This book is for informational and educational purposes only and does not constitute legal advice. The author is not a lawyer and makes no guarantees regarding legal outcomes. Readers should consult qualified legal counsel or trusted advocacy organizations before taking action based on this material.

Cover design by Jim Vincent.

Published by Vincent Press

Printed and distributed by IngramSpark

Printed in 2025 • VP Edition 1.2.is

ISBN 978-1-7641693-1-8 (paperback)

For more information, visit: https://jimvincent.us

"Hope is not a lottery ticket you sit on the sofa holding. It is an axe you break down doors with in an emergency."
 —Rebecca Solnit

This is that emergency. Pick up the axe.

CONTENTS

	Prologue	1
	Preface	5
	Preface to the Expanded Edition	7
1.	The Collapse of the Constitutional Promise	9
2.	The Broken Promises of Democracy	13
3.	From Collapse to Country Again	21
4.	Phase I: Defense – Holding the LIne	29
5.	Phase II: Resistance — Expose, Delay, Prepare	37
6.	Phase III: Restoration — The Agenda to Rebuild Democracy	45
7.	Phase IV: Redemption — Delivering What Democracy Was Meant to Provide	53
8.	Phase V: Reinstitution — The Return to Restraint	63
9.	The Responsibility of Power	71
	Appendix A: The Restoration Agenda: 18 Structural Reforms to Rebuild a Fair Democracy	77
	Appendix B: The Redemption Agenda – Fixing What No Longer Works	81
	Appendix C: How to Be Ready When the Knock Comes	85
	Appendix D: Personal Readiness – Legal, Digital, and Emergency Preparation	91
	Reader's Guides	99
	Afterword: Begin Here—The Republic Will Not Restore Itself	135
	Colophon	137
	Also by Jim Vincent	139
	About the Author	141

PROLOGUE

WRITING WHILE THE COUNTRY FELL APART

---◆---

I didn't start out writing a book. I started out trying to tell the truth.

During the 2024 campaign, I was overwhelmed—not by Trump himself, but by the lies I saw being shared by people I had known for decades. On Facebook, in comment threads and reposted memes, I watched a flood of disinformation wash over people I once trusted. It wasn't just spin or exaggeration. It was something deeper, darker—conspiracies dressed up as concern, propaganda packaged as patriotism, and outright character assassination aimed first at Biden, then Harris. The statistics were false. The language was foreign. But the voices were familiar. And it wasn't coming from strangers. It was coming from friends.

So I did what many of us did. I researched. I posted sources. I wrote long, careful replies. I tried to pull people back with facts, with context, with evidence. I asked questions. I asked for sources. I tried to hold the line against the rising tide of deceit. It didn't work. For every falsehood answered, three more would take its place. The work was exhausting. And it was costly. Friends I had known for thirty years became angry—because I questioned what they posted, because I asked them to back it up. I was called names. I was sworn at. I was insulted, mocked, and attacked. Then they blocked me.

That's when I stopped commenting on their posts and started writing my own. At first it was just a way to stay sane. I tracked what had been said, what had been done, and began asking questions no one else seemed to be asking. Why would Trump float buying Greenland or taking over the Panama Canal? Why was Justice Alito asking for favors? Why was Elon Musk handed control of DOGE, and how did it build his private wealth? I wasn't trying to go viral. I was trying to make sense of a country being taken apart. And when something finally held together—when a pattern emerged—I wrote it down and shared it.

Many of those posts were shared dozens of times. Some were shared hundreds. A few, thousands. In three months, my following more than doubled. But with each day's headlines came something new—another outrage, another contradiction. Immigration one day. A crypto grift the next. Tariffs imposed, reversed, reimposed. Then lawsuits. Executive orders. Collapsing agencies. Rising threats. Funds withheld. Generals fired. Career civil servants pushed out. Another loyalist nominated. Another incompetent confirmed. There was no pattern—only noise. I couldn't get ahead of it. I couldn't even keep up.

I began to realize that chaos was the point. It wasn't an accident of incompetence—it was the product of a strategy.

So I stopped reacting and started asking better questions. Why the chaos? Who benefits? What hides inside it? That's when something shifted. Because beneath the mess, one thing was becoming clear: Trump's support was eroding. Not just in one poll or one state—but across the country. The ground was moving. And yet no one was offering a plan—not for what to do next, and not for what to do now.

If there was a strategy, it was buried. Every conversation I saw stayed locked in the latest harm, the latest fire, the latest lie. We saw courage—Cory Booker's 25-hour filibuster, the Hands Off protests, a growing number of people in the streets—but no shared direction. No coordination. No public blueprint. No map out of the damage and into repair. No vision of what democracy could still become. Still, no plan. If no one else would draw it, I would start with one line.

American Renewal was born not out of certainty, but necessity. Not out of optimism, but refusal—a refusal to let this collapse go unchallenged. A refusal to stay silent. I saw five phases. First, defense: hold what ground we still have. Second, resistance: expose the damage, delay the regime, prepare. Third, restoration: rebuild the broken institutions. Fourth, redemption: fulfill the promises that were broken—justice, liberty, belonging, and trust. Fifth, reinstitution: make sure this never happens again..

This is not the only plan. It may not even be a good plan. But it is a beginning. Start where you can. Start while there's still time. Just start.

I didn't write this because I had time. I wrote it because the country is being dismantled in front of us, and no one I saw had laid out how we survive it—or how we rebuild what will be lost when we do.

So I kept writing. And I'll keep writing—until the crisis ends, the damage is repaired, and democracy is alive again. Or I run out of words.

PREFACE

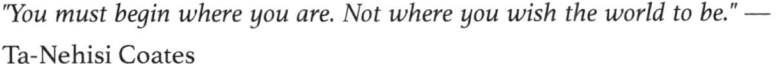

"You must begin where you are. Not where you wish the world to be." —
Ta-Nehisi Coates

The nation is not falling apart in theory. It is collapsing in real time. Not from foreign attack, but from decisions made daily inside its own government—laws ignored, agencies defunded, dissent punished, and public trust ground to ash. Freedoms once assumed —of speech, press, protest, privacy—are being narrowed, not expanded. Power is hoarded. Accountability is mocked. A system designed for balance has become an instrument of dominance.

The six promises of the Constitution—union, justice, tranquility, defense, welfare, liberty—have not been amended. They have been abandoned. In their place stands a government that punishes the disloyal, rewards the powerful, and erodes the rights of those with the least protection. Agencies once built to serve the people now serve the president. Courts once trusted to enforce limits now excuse excess. And citizens once shielded by law now find that law is wielded against them.

Yet none of this was inevitable. What is broken was broken by design—and what was designed can be redesigned. *American Renewal* is not nostalgia for a vanished past. It is a plan to recover the function, fairness, and legitimacy that democracy requires. It is not a platform or a slogan. It is a blueprint for resistance, restoration, and redemption—grounded in law, driven by moral clarity, and built for a moment in which delay means defeat.

What follows is a strategy in four parts. The first lays out the crisis—how democracy has been captured not by coup, but by process. The second maps the path forward—what must happen, and when, if we are to escape permanent minority rule. The third presents the Restoration Agenda: eighteen structural reforms to rebuild a democracy that counts every vote, checks executive power, ensures judicial integrity, and upholds public trust. The fourth presents the Redemption Agenda: eighteen policy outcomes that no functioning republic can afford to ignore—ranging from child care and climate to digital security, fair taxation, and protection from foreign interference.

These reforms are not exhaustive. But they are essential. None are optional. And none can wait. This plan does not pretend to solve every problem. It begins with what must be true if the promises of the Constitution are to mean something again.

We begin here—not with idealism, but with intent. Not with fear, but with resolve. Not with the leaders we wish we had, but with the people still willing to rise. What follows is not a partisan platform. It is a reckoning—and a roadmap. Because if democracy is to survive, it will not be saved by tradition, or memory, or myth. It will be saved by us.

PREFACE TO THE EXPANDED EDITION

───── ✦ ─────

This volume began as a warning. It has become an archive of the collapse—and a manual for recovery. Since its first publication, what was forecast has come to pass. The safeguards failed. The courts retreated. The presidency, unconstrained by law or consequence, has accelerated its assault on the institutions it once swore to preserve. The Expanded Edition exists because the danger has deepened, and so must our understanding—and our response.

What remains unchanged is the purpose. The American Renewal project was never about nostalgia. It was a commitment to clarity, to law, and to the unshakable idea that democracy must function if it is to endure. This edition adds only what necessity demands: deeper documentation, clearer tools, and guidance for those who must now act with greater urgency than ever before. What follows is not a new plan. It is the same roadmap, sharpened for harder terrain.

To support the work ahead, we have added Reader's Guides to

each chapter. They are not summaries, but invitations: to reflect, to act, and to carry the chapter's meaning beyond its final line.

The republic was not built for ease. It was built for perseverance. So is this book.

1

THE COLLAPSE OF THE CONSTITUTIONAL PROMISE

HOW AMERICAN IDEALS WERE ABANDONED FOR POWER, PROFIT, AND PATRONAGE

———✦———

"We the People of the United States, in Order to form a more perfect Union, establish Justice, ensure domestic Tranquility, provide for the common defence, promote the general Welfare, and secure the Blessings of Liberty to ourselves and our Posterity, do ordain and establish this Constitution for the United States of America." — Preamble to the U.S. Constitution

One hundred days into Donald Trump's second term, the collapse of American governance is no longer a forecast. It is daily fact. The stock market convulses with each announcement—tariffs imposed, reversed, then imposed again. Over two hundred lawsuits have already been filed. More than one hundred executive orders have been signed, many unconstitutional, several already blocked. Agencies have been gutted. Career officials dismissed. The Department of Justice now serves the president's interests. Five major laws have passed—each one drafted behind closed doors, and nearly all along party lines.

None of this is accidental. It is the culmination of a slow unraveling. But it is the Constitution that provides the clearest measure of what has been lost. Its preamble outlines six duties: to form a more perfect union, establish justice, ensure domestic tranquility, provide for the common defense, promote the general welfare, and secure the blessings of liberty. These are not vague ideals. They are the foundational promises of self-government. Each one has been broken.

We are not forming a more perfect union. We are splintering into parallel nations. Red states pass laws to defy federal rules. Blue states build parallel systems to shield their citizens from federal overreach. Partisan gerrymandering has severed the link between votes and outcomes. Federal power is now used to intimidate dissent, reward loyalty, and deepen division. Maps are rigged. Votes are suppressed. Oversight mechanisms—the inspectors general, watchdogs, and whistleblower protections that once ensured institutional accountability—have been hollowed out or silenced. The tools meant to defend the republic have been turned against it.

We are not establishing justice. We are watching its selective enforcement. Federal prosecutors shield the president's allies while targeting his critics. Judges ignore precedent in favor of ideology. The Supreme Court—with justices who vacation with billionaires and rule on cases involving their benefactors—no longer enforces limits. It removes them. Legal standards are rewritten to serve power, not law. Section 3 of the Fourteenth Amendment—meant to bar insurrectionists from office—remains unimplemented. The promise that no one is above the law has become a punchline. The courts still wear robes. But justice has taken sides.

Domestic tranquility has been replaced by deliberate chaos. Mass arrests follow mass protests. Orders are issued to provoke resistance, then used to justify harsher crackdowns. Surveillance is expanded. Speech is chilled. Inside this administration, turmoil is not a failure of leadership. It is the governing method. Emergency powers—once reserved for national peril—are declared with abandon, bypassing Congress and concentrating power in the presidency. Each crisis becomes an opportunity to suspend limits, sidestep law, and consolidate control.

The common defense, once a shared national interest, now bends to personal loyalty. Military leaders are dismissed for perceived disloyalty. NATO is undermined. Intelligence briefings are twisted for propaganda or ignored entirely. Cybersecurity teams have been purged. Infrastructure remains vulnerable to both foreign infiltration and domestic sabotage. Foreign interference is no longer hypothetical—it is enabled. American sovereignty is compromised not by invasion, but by complicity. The line between national defense and political survival has all but vanished.

The general welfare has been sacrificed to oligarchy. Policies are designed not to serve the public, but to extract from it. Public education, housing, and health are targeted for privatization. Agencies that regulate polluters or protect workers are handed to industry insiders. The tax code is engineered to preserve generational wealth and shield billionaires. A fair economy is replaced by a feudal one. Even basic supports—child care, nutrition, paid leave—are treated as luxuries rather than guarantees. The result is not freedom. It is dependence on the goodwill of the powerful.

And the blessings of liberty? They are conditional. Protesters are jailed. Journalists are surveilled. Women are prosecuted for medical care. Students are silenced. Immigrants are targeted. In some states, the right to vote has become a bureaucratic gauntlet. In others, the outcome is predetermined before a single vote is cast. Freedom of speech remains on paper. But freedom from retaliation has vanished. The language of liberty is used to justify its removal.

The collapse is not complete. But it is accelerating. And if we are to reverse it, we must begin with clarity. The system is not malfunctioning. It is performing exactly as it has been redesigned to do—by those who benefit from impunity, inequality, and control. Reversing this collapse will require more than new leaders. It will require new structures—restoration not just of policy, but of the very conditions that allow democracy to function.

That is the purpose of what follows. The next chapter lays out the structural blueprint for democratic repair. The one after that defines what redemption must look like in practice—how a functional republic begins to make good on its broken promises. Not just opportunity, but fairness. Not just access, but trust restored. Reforms that protect children, uphold dignity in work, defend truth as foundational, and return government to its rightful role: a servant of the people, not a weapon against them.

The constitutional promises were never meant to be ornamental. They were meant to be delivered. This chapter documents their collapse. The rest of this book is how we rebuild them.

2

THE BROKEN PROMISES OF DEMOCRACY

HOW MINORITY RULE REPLACED MAJORITY CONSENT

———— ✦ ————

"The liberty of democracy is not safe if the people tolerate the growth of private power to a point where it becomes stronger than their democratic state itself."— Franklin D. Roosevelt

Democracy in the United States is broken. Not in metaphor. In function. The Constitution defines what government is meant to provide: a more perfect union, justice, domestic tranquility, the common defense, the general welfare, and the blessings of liberty. These are not decorative words. They are the measure of whether democracy is working. Today, those six promises stand violated. Not eroded by time. Not delayed by compromise. Broken—by design, for power. This chapter does not forecast what might go wrong. It documents what already has. Promise by promise, we show how the government has abandoned its purpose—and what that abandonment has made possible.

In what follows, we will examine each of these six promises not as slogans, but as constitutional mandates—through the eyes of the

Framers: what they envisioned, what they intended, and how far we have strayed.

A more perfect union no longer describes the United States. Unity has been replaced by factional dominance. Congress now functions not as a deliberative body but a trench line—fewer than 10% of bills in 2025 passed with bipartisan support. Red states sue blue states. Governors defy federal rulings by decree. Citizens no longer see one another as neighbors in disagreement, but as existential threats. The executive branch has not tried to close this divide—it has widened it. Cities are threatened with funding cuts. University systems lose grants for ideological noncompliance. Civil servants are required to sign loyalty pledges. This is not the evolution of democracy. It is its weaponization.

Trump did not hide this agenda. He campaigned on division. He called Democrats "vermin," described immigrants as animals, and warned his followers that their enemies were "eating the dogs. They're eating the cats." He promised not healing, but vengeance. "I am your retribution," he declared, and shaped an administration around that pledge. Group identity—racial, geographic, political—became a sorting tool for punishment. Republicans in Congress have voted against their own districts to avoid becoming targets. State legislators have disavowed compromise out of fear. When disagreement is punished and loyalty is coerced, the union is no longer imperfect. It is dismembered. Deliberately.

Justice, once the promise of equal accountability, now depends entirely on allegiance. The Department of Justice has become a mechanism for reward and retaliation. Trump's second term began with sweeping pardons: January 6 rioters, Republican officials, family members, campaign donors. Investigations into foreign interference were closed. Regulatory enforcement was suspended for favored corporations. US Attorneys who worked on Trump-related prosecutions were fired or reassigned. Executive Order 14103 bars "disloyal" law firms from federal contracts or premises. Several firms were coerced into billion-dollar pro bono settlements—committing to defend causes selected by the White House. This is not nonpartisan law enforcement. It is the president's legal arm, repurposed to protect allies and punish dissent.

The pattern is now clear. Cases against Trump—federal and state—remain stalled. In Florida, D.C., and Georgia, no trial has moved forward. In the Garcia case, Trump's lawyers defied a Supreme Court order to return a detained citizen to the U.S.—with no consequence. Judges who resist face harassment or arrest. Two sitting justices, Thomas and Alito, have consistently voted to shield the president from legal constraint, even when precedent or jurisdiction argue otherwise. Meanwhile, immigrants, teachers, and protestors are detained without charge. Unacknowledged detention centers in El Salvador now hold at least forty detainees detention centers in El Salvador now house at least forty detainees without hearing or attorney. This is not prosecutorial discretion. It is collapse. Justice has been reversed: from equal protection to selective enforcement, from rule of law to rule of loyalty.

Domestic tranquility has not disappeared. It has been redefined. The Constitution envisioned a government that preserved public peace through trust and fairness. What exists now is the opposite. Protest is constant—over 11 million Americans have participated in daily demonstrations since January 2025. Not one arrest has been made. But the federal response is not dialogue. It is deterrence. Protest zones are cordoned. Surveillance drones track organizers. Teachers in Arizona and Texas are investigated under "loyalty" laws. Facial recognition scans crowds and flags participants for federal databases. This is not order. It is a warning. Tranquility now means submission. Dissent is still legal—but it is watched.

The president has called for protests outside judges' homes, mocked threats against lawmakers, and promised "retribution" at rallies. Governors defy court orders by decree. Armed militias march in state capitals. Federal judges have been doxxed by legislators. The "Law and Order Act" allows indefinite detention for those labeled threats to "institutional integrity"—a term undefined in law. An executive order now indemnifies law enforcement, offering near-total legal protection. Trump has pledged them "immunity from prosecution." Gun violence continues to climb. Congress refuses reform—blocked by the gun lobby and executive veto. This is not tranquility. It is state power, armored and unleashed.

The common defense, as the Framers intended, meant protecting the nation through professional command, trusted alliances, institutional vigilance, and global cooperation. It was not merely a shield against invasion—it was a promise of preparedness, credibility, and peace through strength. That vision no longer holds. Trump has named a former Fox News host as Secretary of Defense. Experienced officers have been fired for the color of their skin, for who promoted them, or for private doubts about illegal orders. Intelligence briefings focus on political risk. NATO withdrawal is not a threat. It is a campaign promise. The president has openly threatened allies—Canada, Greenland, Panama—and pledged to negotiate peace in Ukraine on Vladimir Putin's terms. This is not strategic ambiguity. It is the abandonment of deterrence.

Diplomatic and military infrastructure has been gutted. Ambassadorships are auctioned to donors, influencers, or family members with no regional experience. Critical field posts remain unfilled due to ideological vetting. Cybersecurity coordination with Europe has been frozen. Agencies tasked with defending against covert foreign influence have been defunded or dismantled. DOJ prosecutions of foreign interference have stalled. State election boards report phishing attempts, spoofed databases, and foreign-funded disinformation campaigns—with no federal response. FEMA failed to respond for 72 hours to Hurricane Elias in Louisiana—not because it refused, but because it was unstaffed. Trump's tariffs have targeted both allies and rivals, destabilizing supply chains and accelerating inflation. In 100 days, the administration has weakened our armed forces, fractured our alliances, surrendered cyber readiness, and destroyed the credibility of American defense leadership. What remains is not national security. It is selective protection—driven by grievance, and pledged only to those who comply.

The general welfare, as the Framers intended it, meant a government that invests in its people—ensuring they are educated, healthy, housed, and protected. It was not charity. It was the foundation of civic strength. In other democracies, this principle is taken seriously. A stable society is one where the people trust that their government, however imperfect, is working—however slowly—to make things better. In the United States, that ethic has been reversed. The current administration does not see public well-being as a duty. It sees it as a threat to power—and an opportunity for profit.

That philosophy now defines policy. The "Freedom Budget" slashes funding to HHS, HUD, and the Department of Labor by nearly 50%. OSHA inspections have fallen by 70%. EPA enforcement is at a 30-year low. NIH cancer research funding has been slashed in key areas. Pell Grants have been capped. PBS and NPR eliminated. Social Security remains unfunded beyond 2035, while privatization proposals gain traction.

The tax code favors inherited wealth, offshore capital, and speculative gains—while working families face increased burdens. Proposals to equalize the system are blocked. Thousands of public servants have been fired without cause—replaced by partisan loyalists or left unfilled. The federal education budget has been converted into unrestricted block grants, increasingly funneled to religious academies. Medicaid expansion has been reversed in seven states. The ACA is under attack by officials openly opposed to public healthcare. The result is predictable: higher costs, reduced care, and record levels of medical bankruptcy.

The economy has not merely slowed. It has fractured. Growth is down. Markets swing wildly. Unemployment is up. The dollar has weakened. Wages stagnate while prices soar. Global tariffs have isolated the U.S. and triggered retaliation. Federal investments in infrastructure have been paused or rescinded. There is no coherent economic policy—only volatility, grievance, and improvisation. This is not a government failing to deliver general welfare. It is a government actively withholding it, believing that instability serves its ends. The pattern is simple: if the general welfare can be sold, it will be. And if it cannot be sold, it will be dismantled or ignored.

The blessings of liberty, as the Framers intended, were guarantees—not gifts. They included the right to speak freely, vote freely, move freely, pray—or not—freely, access accurate information, make medical decisions, marry whom you love, raise children as you see fit, and live without surveillance, censorship, or forced conformity. They included the right to privacy—the shield that protected everything else. Today, these guarantees no longer stand. They have been restricted, criminalized, or revoked. Not for all. But for enough to prove the pattern. Liberty has not faded. It has been rewritten.

Freedom of speech is now filtered through executive control. Newly issued executive orders penalize nonprofits for "obstructing national messaging." Teachers and journalists face criminal charges for "institutional disruption." At least three states are prosecuting librarians for hosting interfaith or LGBTQ+ lessons. Protests are surveilled. Immigration applications are screened for political content. A tweet can cost someone their visa. Contractors may now fire employees for "cultural activism"—including wearing Pride pins or attending protests. The First Amendment still exists—but only for those who do not invoke it in dissent.

Voting rights, too, have become a fiction of geography. Section 5 of the Voting Rights Act remains gutted. The John Lewis Act has stalled. More than 3,000 bills have been introduced nationwide to reduce ballot access. In Georgia, Texas, and Wisconsin, voter purges have resumed. In Florida, offering food or water to voters in line is a crime. Provisional ballots are disproportionately discarded in areas with higher concentrations of young and minority voters. Alabama defied a court order to redraw its map. The Supreme Court let it stand. In presidential elections, outcomes hinge on a few battleground states, effectively sidelining millions of voters elsewhere. The right to vote now depends not on citizenship—but on ZIP code.

Even privacy, once considered the core of constitutional liberty, is now treated as a liability. Personal data—medical, financial, employment, and military service records—are now accessed by DOGE through government partnerships and privatized platforms, under the pretense of "government efficiency." These datasets, still protected by federal law, are now accessed and used without consent. Surveillance is not the exception. It is the mechanism. The Constitution did not promise liberty for the compliant. It promised the blessings of liberty—for ourselves and our posterity. Today, those blessings are not merely broken. They are a fiction. A dream. Or worse, a memory.

The Framers envisioned a democracy that would serve the people—of the people, by the people, for the people. To secure it, they wrote six promises into the Constitution. For much of our history, those promises were kept. Imperfectly. Unequally. But they endured. Today, they do not. They have been weakened over decades, but this administration is breaking them outright—strategically, relentlessly, and at speed. Not out of necessity, but for power, for patronage, and for profit. And yet: the republic is not beyond repair. These promises can be kept again. What follows is not just a record of loss. It is a plan for restoration.

3

FROM COLLAPSE TO COUNTRY AGAIN
A PLAN TO DEFEND, RESIST, RESTORE, REDEEM, AND REINSTITUTE AMERICAN DEMOCRACY

---◆---

"There are moments in history when the only crime is not to act." — JP Vincent

The American republic is no longer held together by law, truth, or consent. The constitutional promises—union, justice, tranquility, defense, welfare, and liberty—have collapsed not by erosion, but by force. And yet: it is not beyond repair. Restoration is still possible. But we must act in time, with clarity, and with discipline. Delay no longer means patience—it means surrender. Time has become a political weapon. Every month that passes hardens illegitimate power into permanent control. Every court ruling left unchallenged becomes precedent. Every agency left hollow becomes irrelevant. What was once the friend of American democracy is now its executioner's tool.

This moment demands a plan. Not just outrage, not just opposition—a plan. We must divide the coming years into five distinct phases, each with its own purpose and peril. Phase I is Defense.

Phase II is Resistance. Phase III is Restoration. Phase IV is Redemption. Phase V is Reinstitution. These are not slogans. They are a strategic progression from collapse to country again. And we are already in motion. The defense has begun. The resistance must be prepared. The restoration must be ready the moment we win. And the redemption must make that victory real—before reinstitution makes it lasting.

Phase I: Defense is now. With Republicans in power and the rule of law under siege, the goal is no longer progress—it is survival. Our tools are lawsuits, injunctions, and independent journalism. These are not instruments of change, but of delay. Delay is not a weakness. It is the last moral use of time. The purpose of defense is to stall the consolidation of power long enough for the people to intervene through elections. The courts and the press are our remaining sentinels. We must protect them like endangered species. They are holding the air for us while we surface. We defend now not just to stall collapse, but to give the public time to act. That act must be decisive: win Congress in 2026. It is the bridge from defense to resistance. Without it, there is no next phase.

But the public has a role in defense, too. The courts act only when someone brings a case. The press exposes only what someone reveals. We must support lawsuits, document violations, fund legal defense, protect journalists, and amplify truth. Organizers must build local legal networks, digital security teams, and emergency communication chains. Every video, every affidavit, every act of refusal matters. We defend not just through institutions, but through millions of individual decisions. That is what holds the line: not only judges and journalists, but ordinary people who refuse to comply with illegitimate power—and who stay vigilant when silence would be easier.

Phase II: Resistance begins in 2027—not as a break from Defense, but as its continuation with greater power and reach. We must make it possible by winning both chambers of Congress in

2026—and as many state legislatures as possible. This is not optional. Without control of the House and Senate, we cannot obstruct what must be obstructed or expose what must be revealed. Even without the presidency, a Democratic Congress can investigate, legislate, and prepare. Resistance is not noise—it is targeted action. Investigative hearings. Reform bills. Aggressive oversight. Every failed vote reveals what the regime fears. Every hearing that draws blood shows the public what has been done to them. Republicans have long used legislative failure to define terrain. We must now do the same—on purpose, and at scale. This is how we set the stage for restoration: by making sabotage visible, building legislative truth records, and forcing the regime to govern in daylight.

The power of refusal must also be reclaimed. Republicans have used procedural tactics—holds, filibusters, delays—to grind democracy to a halt. We must now use them to stall authoritarian rule. Coordinated non-cooperation is not abandonment of duty. It is the only duty left when law has been hijacked. We are not obliged to help them govern. Tactical refusal is not sabotage. It is a moral stand. The filibuster they abused can be our shield. The nomination delays they used can be our firewall. If we cannot yet build, we must block. If we cannot yet move forward, we must hold the line.

Phase III: Restoration begins only with a Democratic trifecta—control of the presidency, the House, and the Senate—won in 2028 and inaugurated in January 2029. This is the short window in which real reform becomes possible. The eighteen structural reforms outlined in the Restoration Agenda must be passed—fully or in part—within that narrow span. There is no time for hesitation. Every court ruling, every agency rule, and every state law after 2029 will either entrench minority rule or help dismantle it. Delay means defeat. This is not about adapting to broken systems. It is about replacing them before they become permanent.

Restoration is not just a legislative task—it is a moral reckoning. The court must be expanded. The filibuster must be ended. Presidential immunity must be stripped. Ethics must be enforceable by law. Voting rights must be federal, fair, and fraud-resistant. These are not partisan victories. They are democratic necessities. We are not here to seek advantage—we are here to level the field. But leveling it requires forceful change. The system was not corrupted passively—it will not be repaired passively. Restoration is the battle for the tools themselves. And we will not get a second chance to seize them.

Phase IV: Redemption begins the moment reforms are passed. Restoration wins the tools—but Redemption must prove the system can serve again. This phase is where trust is rebuilt—not through promises, but through results. Government must become visible again—not as spectacle, but as service. Citizens must see clean water, working hospitals, protected rights, honest courts, and secure elections. Redemption is the long, quiet labor of dignity restored. It is not dramatic—but it is decisive. No reform holds without belief. No law lasts without legitimacy. Redemption is not ideology. It is lived fairness. It is the foundation for everything that follows.

Redemption does not end on a schedule. It will continue only as long as the public sees real results—and responds with confidence, renewed engagement, and the return of power. It will span elections. It must survive setbacks. There is no shortcut to sustaining a governing majority. Unlike minority rule, which survives by distortion, Redemption must survive by consent. Every election becomes a test—not just of popularity, but of integrity, delivery, and earned legitimacy. If the work falters, or the public turns away, the restoration will erode. Redemption is not a pause between battles. It is the proof that democracy can work again.

Phase V: Reinstitution begins before Redemption is complete. These reforms are not permanent power grabs—they are corrective measures to restore fairness. But the longer we hold extraordinary tools, the greater the risk they become normalized. That risk must be managed, not ignored. Reinstitution is the slow, deliberate return to restraint. Expand the Court to unrig it—and then return it to a neutral size. End the filibuster—and then replace it with a fairer rule. Reclaim presidential power—and then bind it by law. We are not here to cheat better. We are here to ensure no one can cheat again.

The challenge is timing. Reinstitution must not begin so early that it undermines what has just been built. But it must not begin so late that the habits of emergency harden into tyranny of our own. Restoration gave us tools. Redemption tested them in public. Reinstitution ensures we can step back without collapsing what we've made. It is the final measure of integrity: that we use what was seized to build what is shared—and then, without being forced, relinquish what we no longer need. The test of a republic is not how it wins power, but how—and when—it lets go.

There is a temptation to believe that winning one election will fix this. But no single election can repair a system that has been deliberately corrupted. Without structural reform, any Democratic victory will be temporary—hostage to courts, sabotage, and delay. That is what undid Obama's final years. That is what paralyzed Biden's early ones. But even with reform, success is not guaranteed. Redemption must be earned in the public mind. Reinstitution must be timed with care. If we win and govern poorly—or wait too long to let go—we will lose the trust that makes democracy last. This is our window. And we either break through it—or it becomes a wall.

This plan will not execute itself. It requires leadership—real, prepared, principled leadership—across every branch of government. We need a president who does not manage decline, but ends it. But we also need a Speaker who can unite the caucus and pass a tsunami of bills into law. A Senate Majority Leader with the courage to change the rules and deliver those laws to the Resolute Desk. And we need parallel leadership in the states—governors, secretaries of state, attorneys general, and legislative majorities ready to govern under pressure. Federal laws will set the course. But it is the states that must sail it. This kind of leadership does not emerge by accident. It is built—by movements, by demand, and by a public ready to ask for more than survival.

We know what this kind of leadership looks like—especially when it must come from the top. The president elected in 2028 will inherit not normalcy, but damage. Their role will not be to govern alone, but to lead a government of reformers—legislators, state leaders, judges, and public servants—through a reconstruction of the republic. If Redemption extends beyond their term, the next president must carry the mission forward, not turn back. We've seen this kind of leadership before. Lincoln inherited secession. FDR inherited collapse. Washington inherited revolution. Each refused the limited tools they were given. They did not manage crisis. They refounded the nation in its shadow. The next great American leader must do the same. Not a caretaker. A founder. Someone who sees the past, faces the present, and builds a future that makes tyranny obsolete. They will not be thanked for doing it. But if they do not act, there may be no republic left to thank them.

That leader will need to make impossible choices. End the filibuster. Expand the Court. Strip presidential immunity. Enforce ethics without compromise. They will be called tyrants for dismantling tyranny. They will be hated for ending lawlessness. They will be slandered by the very system they are trying to save. And they must act anyway. Because legitimacy does not come from permission—it comes from doing what must be done. They will not be loved in their moment. But they will be right. And they will be remembered—if they win.

But no leader rises alone. Movements build leaders. Organizers build power. People build possibility. Local officials, secretaries of state, governors, teachers, veterans, and protestors must all be part of this. The next phase of American self-government will not be commanded from Washington. It will be raised from the edges—by those whose integrity has not been purged. If we wait for a single figure to save us, we will lose everything. If we move together, we will build something no one person could ever command.

Movements are made of action. Not admiration. This fight requires civic militancy: door-knockers, fundraisers, poll watchers, lawsuit filers, state-level candidates, digital organizers. This is not the work of politics. It is the work of freedom. Nothing about it will be easy. But everything about it will be necessary. The mistake we made was believing democracy was self-sustaining. It isn't. It must be defended. Rebuilt. Made tangible. Freedom is never won wholesale. It is restored in fragments. And it becomes whole only when enough people hold the line—long enough, and together enough, to make freedom real.

We must also change the message. The old language of passive hope is not enough. We need moral clarity, tactical unity, and cultural resonance. *American Renewal* must become a shorthand—a phrase that means something. Say it on talk shows. Say it in campaign speeches. Say it at school board meetings, in protests, in sermons. A plan not spoken is a plan unknown. And a plan unknown is a plan unfollowed. The plan is here. But it only matters if people recognize it, carry it, and claim it as their own.

American Renewal is not a perfect plan. It is not final. It is not immune to challenge. But it is named. And that is the beginning. You cannot organize what you will not name. You cannot refine what has no shape. You cannot act on what no one will claim. *American Renewal* gives form to something real—flawed, evolving, and shared. That is its value. It invites disagreement. It demands debate. But it also demands action. Until we name what we are fighting for, we will always be fighting only what we are against.

And above all, the public must want it. They must believe again —not just that democracy is possible, but that it is worth fighting for. That it is worth the work. That it is worth the risk. A leader can guide a nation. But only a nation that chooses to move. The plan is not enough. The power is not enough. Only a people awakened can make this real. We do not need another election cycle. We need a national decision.

So ask now—not in 2028, but today: Who among us will lead this? Who will organize it? Who will believe in it when the country has forgotten how? And if no one rises in time, then we must. Not just to vote. Not just to support. But to become the answer ourselves. If we do not rise, the republic will fall. Not all at once. But piece by piece. And it will end not with an explosion, but with a silence. A silence no one bothered to break.

4

PHASE I: DEFENSE – HOLDING THE LINE

BEFORE WE CAN REBUILD DEMOCRACY, WE MUST KEEP IT FROM FALLING. THIS IS HOW WE HOLD THE LINE.

"Everyone. Everywhere. All at once. That's how we hold." — JP Vincent

The American government is no longer functioning as a democracy. The presidency is wielded lawlessly. Congress, though barely Republican, aligns with the regime's will. The courts, while not yet fully captured, are increasingly complicit. We cannot yet advance. But we can slow collapse. We can buy moments. We can hold ground for those preparing to resist. This is Phase I: Defense. It is a calculated, disciplined stand—not designed to win, but to survive. And in this moment, survival is resistance. It is defiance. It is intelligent, persistent, relentless action. Everywhere. All at once.

The outcome of the 2024 election was not a mandate—it was a seizure. Through voter suppression, gerrymandering, and disinformation, Trump secured power without accountability. He governs without majority support and acts without legal constraint. But even authoritarianism has limits. Courts can enjoin unlawful actions.

Investigations can expose corruption. The press can still shine light. Delay is not surrender. Delay is the ground on which we stand. Those who hope for progress must first protect what remains. This is not a normal contest of policies. It is a race between erosion and endurance. And endurance, for now, is all we hold.

Two forces remain capable of slowing the descent: the courts and the press. Both are imperfect. Both are under siege. But they are still functioning. Courts at every level—state, district, federal, even the Supreme Court—have temporarily blocked illegal purges, unlawful deportations, and executive overreach. These rulings would not exist without action: lawsuits filed by civil rights lawyers, legal nonprofits, and state attorneys general. The decisions are not permanent. But they freeze damage. They give movements time to organize, cooperative states time to legislate, and watchdogs time to gather evidence. The press amplifies what the courts cannot reach. And the people—soon—must do what neither can.

These institutions are not eternal. They are not infinite in resilience. The judiciary is under relentless attack—from inside and out. Trump has not yet reshaped the courts, but he has threatened judges, filed retaliatory impeachment articles, mocked the legitimacy of rulings, and removed Justice Department officials he deems disloyal. He ignores court orders with impunity, daring the system to constrain him. Meanwhile, the press faces exclusion, manipulation, and selective access. Major media outlets have been pressured into settlements, staff changes, and editorial retreat. Without lawyers to file suit, judges to rule, journalists to investigate, and uncompromised media to report—it all unravels. And that is the plan.

The courts and the press still function—but only because others make them move. Lawsuits don't file themselves. Sources don't leak on cue. Defense in this phase is not retreat. It is interruption. Legal advocates, public interest groups, and citizens must use every available lever to slow the regime's advance. When authoritarian power depends on speed and spectacle, the first act of resistance is to interrupt the show. We cannot yet govern. But we can disrupt, delay, and expose. Delay is not indecision—it is strategy. Not paralysis, but restraint. Not surrender, but time reclaimed from collapse.

Every injunction filed, every FOIA request submitted, every document leaked into daylight breaks the illusion of inevitability. Even failed cases force disclosures, create records, and expose patterns of abuse. Delay does not stop the machinery—it gums its gears. It grants lawyers time to prepare, activists time to organize, journalists time to publish, and voters time to awaken. This is not legalism. It is a form of siege defense. And it works—if we sustain it. The law will not save us alone. But if we use it relentlessly, it can slow collapse just long enough for democracy to fight its way back.

The press plays a different role: it doesn't slow the machinery—it exposes what it was never meant to reveal. Exposés fracture loyalty. Pattern recognition turns scattered facts into indictment. The regime cannot govern in daylight. Every well-timed report forces reaction: congressional inquiries, court filings, resignations. Journalism is not passive. It is a form of rupture. A captured state cannot survive an uncontrolled narrative. We must support independent reporters, subscribe to serious outlets, and challenge propaganda at its source. In this moment, the press is not a mirror of democracy. It is a weapon for its survival. Wield it. Guard it.

The power of delay is psychological as well as structural. The regime thrives on inevitability—on the myth that nothing can stop it. But when lawsuits are filed, hearings are held, resignations are forced, and rallies flood the streets, inevitability fractures. Delay proves the regime can be fought. And what can be fought can be beaten. That is why delay is dangerous to authoritarianism. It is not the delay itself, but what it enables. On April 5, the protests were ignored. On April 19, they returned—larger, louder, better organized—and landed on the front pages. Delay made notice possible. Delay gives room for courage. It gives time for clarity. It holds the line until others arrive. It is not weakness. It is the refusal to concede.

But defense is not only institutional. When judges and journalists falter—or fall—the burden shifts to the people. That is where grassroots networks must rise. Across the country, resistance is already forming: legal watchdogs, rapid-response protest groups, election monitors, courtwatch volunteers, and citizen-led information networks. When institutions are corrupted, civic action becomes the immune system. And individuals—alert, observant, unafraid—are its sensors. Journalists need witnesses. Every photograph, every video, every firsthand account is a thread in the net that catches abuse. One video of an ICE raid can be ignored. A hundred cannot. We must fund these networks, join them—and if there is none, set one up—and feed them the truth. They are the new sentinels. So are we.

This kind of vigilance—watching, documenting, showing up—must become habit. And habit needs structure. That's where initiatives like FiveFifteen come in. Named for its core premise—that you can commit to five acts of resistance in fifteen days—it isn't about scale. It's about rhythm. Write postcards. Call your representatives. Show up at a town hall. Volunteer as a poll worker. Support a local reporter. Donate to legal aid. Attend a protest. The act itself matters less than the discipline. Resistance must be ritualized. The goal is not just to act—but to become the kind of person who acts. In a system designed to produce passivity, commitment is rebellion. And rebellion is the only road back.

Institutions can slow the collapse. But they cannot prevent it alone. The courts require plaintiffs. The press requires witnesses. And democracy—cornered, besieged, still breathing—requires action from its people. That is where the next line of defense begins. Not in grand gestures, but in disciplined, repeatable acts of resistance. What follows are not theories. They are acts of democratic resistance. If you've ever asked, "But what can I do?"—this is your answer.

One such movement is FiveFifteen—named for its premise: that you can commit to five acts of resistance in fifteen days. It is not about scale. It is about habit. Write postcards. Call your representatives. Show up at a town hall. Volunteer as a poll worker. Support a local reporter. Donate to legal aid. Attend a protest. The act itself matters less than the discipline. Resistance must be ritualized. The purpose is not just to act—but to become the kind of person who acts. In a system designed to produce passivity, commitment is rebellion. And rebellion is the only road back.

Another form of resistance is collective noncooperation. The movement known as Immovable helps people organize legal, nonviolent acts of disruption—walkouts, slowdowns, coordinated absences, and refusals to implement unlawful policies. These tactics don't require confrontation. But they do require coordination. A single absence is overlooked. Hundreds delay enforcement. Thousands can freeze a rollout. These actions do not overthrow regimes —but they interrupt the machinery. And interruption buys time. Not everyone can participate directly. But those who can should. And those who can't can support the ones who do. In a captured state, even hesitation is a form of defiance. And organized hesitation becomes power. For more tools, groups, and guides, see Appendix C: Civic Resistance – Tools, Networks, and Tactics for Phase I: Defense.

But resistance is not only about exposure or delay. It is also about protection. In every authoritarian regime, certain communities are hit first and hardest—immigrants, dissidents, religious minorities, LGBTQ citizens, civil servants. If you are not among them, your role is to shield them. That means organizing accompaniment for ICE encounters. It means court support. It means jail visits. It means amplifying their stories and physically showing up. These actions do not make headlines. But they save lives. They keep families together. They buy days, weeks, months—enough to mount a legal challenge or move to safety. This, too, is defense.

Personal preparation is part of this phase. If they come for you—

or someone you love—you must be ready. That means knowing your rights, securing your documents, backing up your files, naming legal contacts, and sharing passwords with a trusted ally. None of these acts are signs of panic. They are signs of readiness. Being prepared is not paranoia. It is solidarity. Appendix D: Personal Readiness – Legal, Digital, and Emergency Preparation for Phase I: Defense offers a full checklist. If thousands take these steps, we become harder to intimidate, harder to erase, harder to silence. The regime relies on fear. Preparation breaks its spell. It tells them: You may come, but we are not afraid.

But we must also resist the traps laid to drain us. Authoritarianism feeds on outrage and distraction. It wants us to be exhausted, scattered, reactive. Don't give it that victory. Stay informed—but limit your intake. Choose a reliable news source. Check headlines once or twice a day. Then log off. Focus your time on action, not obsession. Pick one issue—immigration, healthcare, the environment, voting rights—and contribute meaningfully. Don't argue online with trolls or waste hours convincing the unconvincible. Your time is too precious. Your talents too needed. Leave the door open—but don't wait for those who refuse to walk through.

In an age of engineered chaos, distraction is a weapon. One day, Trump posts an image of himself as pope. Outrage floods the feed—while citizens are still being kidnapped off the street. A week later, Pete Hegseth brings his wife to a classified briefing; for a moment, we forget that funds are being withheld from major research institutions. A 100% tariff on foreign films dominates headlines—while Musk retains the private medical, financial, and employment records of millions. This is not sloppiness. It is strategy. Don't follow the chaos. Stay with what matters. Choose your issue. Track the facts. Plan your actions. Let the rest go.

While national headlines dominate, it is your state legislature that draws district maps, passes voter laws, and restricts or expands rights. That is where the next coup will be formalized—or stopped.

Know your state legislators. Know how they vote. Track what they say—publicly, in session, and in response to your questions. Attend their town halls. Demand action. They are often more vulnerable to pressure than members of Congress. They know you live nearby. They know their margin of victory may be small enough that even a few disappointed voters can end their careers. This is not about threats. It is about consequence. Make accountability unavoidable. And visible.

Members of Congress, too, can be moved. Many are afraid—of Trump, yes, but not for reasons of principle or policy. They fear his ability to unleash a primary challenger. They fear being turned into a viral punchline, a late-night monologue, a target of MAGA rage. Their fear is political death. Let them fear the alternative: public, organized, relentless democratic pressure. Protest at their offices. Flood their inboxes. Show up at their town halls. Ask the question: "Do you stand by what he did—or were you just silent?" Let them know their silence is not free. If they won't lead, make them follow. If they won't follow, make them fear their seat. This, too, is nonviolent defense.

Some readers will say: this is too much. I'm just one person. That's true. And that's exactly why this works. No one can do everything. But everyone can do something. Make a sign. Start a group. Write a letter. Run for school board. Host a voter registration table. Raise $100 for legal aid with a lemonade stand. Pick one thing. Pick one issue. Pick one candidate. Then go to FiveFifteen.com and commit to five things in the next fifteen days—or set your own schedule, define your own domain, and make your actions a habit. The only act that will fail is doing nothing. Start now. Stay in motion. Let it become who you are.

Phase I: Defense is not glamorous. It is not transformative. But it is essential. It is the work of those who hold the air while others surface. It is how we remain free long enough to restore freedom. It is not a speech. It is a trench. Every act of legal delay, journalistic exposure, civic resistance, and quiet readiness is a stake in the ground. It is a line drawn not in ideology but in survival. If we lose this phase, there will be no second. But if we hold it—just long enough—we begin again. And once we begin, we can become unstoppable. Everyone. Everywhere. All at once. That's how we hold.

5

PHASE II: RESISTANCE — EXPOSE, DELAY, PREPARE

WHEN RESTORATION IS NOT YET POSSIBLE, RESISTANCE BECOMES THE DUTY. THE PRESSURE MUST CONTINUE. THE FIGHT MUST WIDEN.

———◆———

"We could not restore what was lost. Not yet. But we made sure it was seen. And we made sure it did not get worse." — Heather Cox Richardson

Trump controls the presidency. The Supreme Court shields him. The Republican Congress enables him. The agencies of state have been turned against their purpose and to his. And the only chance to stop this descent is more than a year away. If we do not take back the House and Senate in 2026, the regime will face no internal resistance. There will be no investigations. No oversight. No procedural brakes. No dissent inside government. And if Trump holds unchecked power for four years, democracy may not recover.

But the tide has started to turn. Not just in anger. Not just in protests, But in elections. In Florida's 1st and 6th congressional districts—deep red districts where Republicans were expected to cruise—both GOP candidates underperformed by margins that stunned even their own internal pollsters. In Wisconsin, despite Elon Musk's lottery campaign and tens of millions in donations, the Trump-backed candidate for Supreme Court lost by ten points. In Canada, the Trump-aligned party collapsed—losing a 10-point lead and falling 15 points behind in just ninety days. In Australia, the Liberal Party, also Trump-aligned, suffered its worst defeat in a generation. The pattern is clear: the people are waking up. And voting.

The urgent task now is to turn that awaking, that anger, those votes to a win in 2026. And once Democrats control Congress, the task is not to legislate. It is to resist. We will not be governing in the traditional sense. We will be exposing what has been hidden, delaying what cannot be stopped, and preparing for a restoration that is not yet possible. The presidency will still be lawless. The courts will still be captured. But Congress, if unified, can become a blockade and a beacon. The years that follow must be relentless, courageous, and clear.

Even with that victory, we will still have lost the presidency, the courts, and the executive agencies. Congress is the last institutional place where power can still be claimed of, by and for the people. If we cannot take it back, there is no check. No pause. No delay. That is what 2026 decides—not the future of legislation, but whether government can be made to serve the people at all. To save democracy, we must win in 2026.

Democratic control of both chambers will not be enough. Nothing we pass will become law. Every protection we propose—reproductive freedom, voting rights, civil liberties, press independence—will be vetoed. But that is the point. We write bills to show the country what it could have had. We legislate to reveal what this regime denies. Each veto becomes a confession. Each refusal, a campaign ad. And every hearing, every investigation, every document subpoenaed becomes a window into the crimes and cowardice that have been buried in silence. This is not governance. It is resistance by legislation.

These years must be used to delay what cannot yet be defeated. That means stalling nominations, defunding implementation, mandating oversight, and forcing review. It means legislative landmines—procedures that trigger delays, hearings that slow appointments, amendments that tie enforcement to transparency. Republicans used these tools for sabotage. We now use them for survival. Delay is not dysfunction. Delay is time. And time is the one thing authoritarianism cannot abide without full control.

Every hold is an act of resistance. Every amendment that slows confirmation is a line drawn. The filibuster, the calendar, the markup session—all of it becomes a means to defend what cannot yet be rescued. If we use these tools with purpose, we do not just frustrate the regime. We show the public that someone inside the building still understands what the stakes are.

But delay alone is not enough. We must listen to the people who gave us this chance. Every town hall must be a forum, not a performance. Every congressional speech, every congressional vote must be tied to their struggle. These two years are a test. The public must see that someone inside the government is still fighting for them. And they must see that our resistance is not performance—it is representation. It is what they demanded when they gave us the House. When they gave us the Senate.

If we do not listen to the people, we will lose them. We will again be the party of strongly-worded letters and disappointment. Just another party of betrayal. We cannot afford that. Not morally. Not politically. Not historically. These two years are our second chance—and our last. Everything must be earned. Everything must be exposed. Everything must be slowed until we regain public trust—so we can change it all for good.

These years must also expose the movement behind the man. Trump is not alone. He is the face of a project decades in the making

—a plan to erode institutions, corrupt loyalty, and dismantle dissent. A plan to reward obedience and punish truth. A plan to ultimately erase democracy itself. The Republican senators and representatives who refused to stop him are still in office. The donors who funded it are now collecting their rewards—at public expense. The media figures who excused it still broadcast lies every night.

This exposure is not about one man. It is about a machine. And the new Congress must make it visible—day after day, night after night. Without quarter. Without pause. That includes naming those who stayed silent. The bureaucrats who enforced unlawful orders. The agencies that bent to pressure. The donors who paid tribute and reaped spoils. The courts and justices who ruled with one eye closed.

This is not a purge. It is a record. If the system will not hold these men and women accountable, then history must. And we must write that record—into the Congressional Record, into every remaining newsroom that still tells the truth, and into the public conscience, where it cannot be erased. And will be remembered.

The judiciary must not be spared scrutiny. Trump's captured Supreme Court has dominated headlines, but hundreds of lower court judges—many appointed for ideological loyalty—now shape immigration, policing, voting access, and education. Their rulings must be documented. Their conflicts of interest must be investigated. Their impact must be mapped. But naming them is only the beginning. Most are bound by formal ethics rules. Some are elected. All are subject to public scrutiny.

No regime survives compromised judges. And no restoration will succeed if such judges remain unchallenged. We must act—not just to expose them, but to weaken their hold on the future.

These two years must also be the time when a leader for Restoration and Redemption begins to emerge—not chosen in secret, but forged in public. From the hearings. From the town halls. From the floor fights. From the courage to say what others will not.

The Democratic nominee in 2028 cannot be a compromise. They must be a fighter. A unifier. Someone who understands not only what was broken, but how to repair it. Someone willing to rebuild what Trump destroyed—and to renew what decades of his party laid to waste. That time must also prepare not just an agenda, but a leader bold enough, strong enough, and popular enough to complete it.

The selection of this leader cannot be staged, faked, or left to chaos. They must earn it—in the field, on the floor, in the town halls, even in the news and sound bites. But if no leader rises quickly, the party must have the discipline to choose one—based not on seniority or ambition, but on charisma, judgment, intelligence, public trust, and a proven record of getting things done. We cannot afford another primary season of mutual destruction. In 2016, flaws exposed in debate became weapons in the general election—used not by Democrats, but by Trump himself.

The public does not demand perfection. But they do demand someone they can trust—and proof that the party is united behind them. They will follow strength if they see it, and abandon it if we tear ourselves apart.

That unity must begin now. The work ahead is too urgent for internal posturing. If these years are to matter, Democrats must stand as one: different strategies, yes, but one mission. This is not the time for positioning or purity tests. It is the time to build. The country is watching. So is history.

When unity is secured, the real work begins. This is the task: use every inch of power to delay the regime, expose its enablers, support the resistance, restore public trust, and prepare the country to retake itself. That means flipping state legislatures, fortifying election systems, documenting the crimes already committed, building alliances, and preparing prosecutions that begin the moment power shifts. We must not only imagine restoration. We must scaffold it while we resist.

The defensive actions that got us through 2025 and 2026 must continue through 2027 and 2028. The personal protections. The legal readiness. The mutual defense of journalists, teachers, immigrants, workers, students, doctors, and organizers. These cannot stop. They must expand. They must intensify. Even with control of Congress, we cannot relax. Just because we gained seats does not mean we gained safety. The knock still comes. The raids still happen. Surveillance still spreads. The threats are still real. The corruption, the grift, the targeting, the dismantling, and the defunding have not stopped.

Trump is still in power. And he is trying to stay there. This phase of resistance is not a transition. It is a continuation—with a few more levers, a few more tools, and a few more seats to use in the fight.

And with these levers and tools, we show the country what it looks like to fight with power and restraint. To resist with discipline. To honor the trust that was given not because we were loved, but because we were needed—because we listened, clearly and without delay. We do not confuse manners for morality. We do not confuse compromise for progress. We act because the moment demands it—and because delay, or silence, or disunity is no longer survivable.

But this is not Congress's job alone. You are needed. Just as in the phase of defense, the phase of resistance requires everyone—everywhere, all at once, tirelessly. What we hold depends on how widely it is defended, how quickly truth is spoken, and how visibly solidarity appears. Organize your state. Train your precinct. Protect your community. Show up at the town hall. Speak the truth into public silence. Share what you know. Name what you see. The next phase of this resistance lives wherever people refuse to let democracy fall—and if you're unsure where to begin, Appendix D offers tools to help you start, strengthen, and sustain your contributions.

This phase is not where we repair what was broken. It is where we stop the bleeding and reveal the wound. With Congress, we slow the destruction and bring sabotage into the light. With a leader, we prepare for what must follow. With unity, we prove that the resistance is more than survival—it is discipline, visibility, and truth. This phase is not a replacement for the last. It is its continuation and its expansion. We must win Congress in 2026. But even that will not be enough. Resistance now belongs to every seat in Congress and every street in the country. The job is not only to delay collapse. It is to prove—through courage, coherence, and clarity—that the country can still be made whole again.

6

PHASE III: RESTORATION — THE AGENDA TO REBUILD DEMOCRACY

EIGHTEEN REFORMS TO RESTORE CONSTITUTIONAL DEMOCRACY

―――― ✦ ――――

"While the Constitution protects against invasions of individual rights, it is not a suicide pact." — Justice Arthur Goldberg, Kennedy v. Mendoza-Martinez (1963)

We have lived too long in a democracy by illusion—a system where elections are held but rigged through maps; where judges wear robes but rule like partisans; where the people still vote, but the outcomes are foregone. We tell ourselves the republic remains because the rituals continue. But rituals without fairness are not democracy. They are performance. And performance cannot protect a people from tyranny. If we want to govern ourselves again, we must rebuild the structures that make self-government possible.

This chapter is the turning point—the moment where resistance becomes design, and protest becomes plan.

This is not a revolution. It is repair. The American system was never designed for minority rule, but it has been twisted to deliver exactly that. The Electoral College allows a president to govern without winning the people. The Senate gives veto power to rural states. The Supreme Court, captured by ideology, blocks reform even when passed by overwhelming consensus. And the rules of elections—who can vote, how votes are counted, which votes matter—are set by those who benefit from fewer votes. These are not accidents. They are outcomes by design.

The eighteen reforms that follow make up the Restoration Agenda. Together, they represent a blueprint—not to win the next election, but to rebuild a government capable of fulfilling the promises of the Constitution. These are not policy prescriptions. They are outcome targets. Each paragraph describes what a functioning democracy should provide—and what is required to get there. Spanning elections, executive power, the courts, and the civic trust, these reforms form the scaffolding of a republic rebuilt. Future chapters will explore each one in depth. But here, we begin with the map.

I. Elections That Count Every Voice

Campaign Finance Reform

Democracy is not a bidding war. And yet today, elections are won not by ideas but by the highest bidder. Unlimited dark money floods every race, shaping outcomes and silencing challengers. Reform means restoring transparency, ending secret funding, setting limits, and creating financing options that allow ordinary Americans to run and win. Candidates should serve voters, not donors. Until we reclaim that principle, elections are auctions—and democracy is for sale.

Voting Rights

In a just democracy, the right to vote is sacred. In today's America, it is strategic. Laws are rewritten to suppress turnout. Voter rolls are purged, polling places closed, ballots discarded. Gerrymandered legislatures write rules to entrench themselves. Reform means restoring the right to vote—securely, universally, and without obstruction. Every citizen should be registered. Every vote should be counted. And no one should fear losing their vote for lack of paperwork or excess of melanin.

Electoral College

The Electoral College served a purpose in the 18th century—when distance, isolation, and limited information made direct national elections impractical. But today, it allows a candidate to win the presidency while losing the popular vote, distorting representation and magnifying the influence of a handful of battleground states. Most Americans know their vote will not sway the outcome, and most presidential campaigns know which voters they must woo and which they can afford to ignore. The result is a system that prizes geography over democracy. Reform must create a national election in which every vote counts equally. A possible starting point is the National Popular Vote Compact—but the principle, not the mechanism, must lead.

Gerrymandering

Gerrymandering breaks the connection between people and power. Districts are drawn to entrench the majority party, not represent communities. The result is distorted outcomes—where the minority can rule and the majority is locked out. Reform must restore fairness. Elections should be earned with character and platform, not engineered by party committee. Until maps are honest, a democracy of the people, by the people, for the people is impossible.

Election Integrity

The phrase "election integrity" has become a justification for destroying the very trust it once represented. The systems and processes that for decades protected ballots and certified results are now being converted into tools of suppression: false audits, targeted purges, and politicized delays. Officials who defend the process face threats. Those who sabotage it are rewarded. Real reform begins with a principle: elections must be fair, uncorruptible, and above all, trusted. That means protecting administrators, securing infrastructure, preventing interference, and honoring the results—no matter who wins.

II. Checks on Presidential Power

Presidential Accountability

Presidents are not kings. And yet today, the presidency is cloaked in impunity. Legal scholars debate whether a president can order assassinations or stage coups without consequence. Executive orders override congressional law. Agencies are used to settle scores and deliver favors. Reform must restore the presidency to its constitutional boundaries. No individual—no matter how elected—is above the law.

Oversight Independence and Protection

Create removal protections and term limits for Inspectors General. Criminalize retaliation against protected whistleblowers. Enforce timely compliance with lawful subpoenas. A government cannot police itself if every investigator can be fired, ignored, or punished. Oversight must be immune from political retaliation—and accountable only to law, not to loyalty.

Emergency Powers

Presidential emergency powers were designed for crisis—not convenience. But in recent years, declarations have become routine—invoked to bypass Congress and impose tariffs, deploy troops, or redirect funds. True reform means restoring oversight. No emergency power should be indefinite. No sweeping authority should rest on a signature. Time limits, court review, and legislative reauthorization must become the norm—not the exception.

Executive Orders

Executive orders are meant to implement policy—not invent it.

But today, they are used to override law, sideline Congress, and erase precedent. Reform must distinguish administration from legislation. Major orders—those affecting rights, spending, or institutional structure—must face automatic review. A government that governs by memo is not a republic. It is a monarchy with better branding.

Pardon Power

The power to pardon was designed for mercy—not protection. But in recent years, it has shielded co-conspirators, bought silence, and obstructed justice. Reform must impose transparency. Self-pardons must be banned. Crony pardons must be exposed. The president may forgive. But he may not forgive himself—or erase the crimes of his enablers.

III. A Judiciary that Upholds Law, Not Loyalty

Judicial Reform

A republic cannot survive without a credible court. But today, trust in the judiciary has collapsed. Supreme Court justices serve for life—confirmed by senates that represent a minority of Americans. Lower courts face crushing backlogs. Ethics are optional. Reform means term limits, expanded benches, and binding rules of conduct. A justice system without justice is a constitutional contradiction.

Section 3 Enforcement

The Fourteenth Amendment bars insurrectionists from holding office. It is not a suggestion. It is a requirement. But Congress has refused to enforce it—and courts claim they cannot without statute. The result is law in limbo. Reform means codifying a process for disqualification. No one who wages war on democracy should be trusted to lead it.

Transparency and Oversight

Democracy dies in darkness. But the Freedom of Information Act is broken. Delays are endless. Exemptions are abused. Private contractors escape scrutiny. Inspectors general and agency watchdogs are dismissed for doing their jobs. Reform must bring transparency into the digital age. Deadlines must be real. Penalties must be enforced. Oversight leaders must be protected from political interference. And privatized governance must be subject to public accountability. Power exercised in secret is power abused.

IV. Rebuilding an Informed Public

Disinformation and Media

The First Amendment protects speech. It does not protect deception. Today's information landscape is dominated by algorithmic manipulation, state propaganda, viral falsehood, and manufactured outrage. Reform means creating a civic information standard: transparent algorithms, verified political ads, and accountability for licensed broadcasters. Truth must be louder than lies. And propaganda must not be funded by the public it misleads.

Civic Literacy

No democracy can survive if its citizens don't understand how it works. Civic literacy is now dangerously low. Americans do not know the branches of government, the role of Congress, or how a bill becomes law. Reform means more than education—it means empowerment. National service programs, civic curricula, and political apprenticeships must make self-government not just a right, but a skill.

This is the Restoration Agenda

These are not partisan demands. They are democratic foundations. Each reform targets a structural failure that, left unchecked, ensures minority rule and democratic decay. None are optional. Each is required—not to secure partisan victory, but to restore constitutional function.

We will return to each reform in full detail—exploring how we arrived here, what's broken, and what solutions might best deliver the outcomes described. This list may not cover every reform democracy will need. But it names the ones we cannot do without.

These reforms will not finish the work. They will make it possible. Once democracy is restored, we can begin the deeper task: to renew the country itself. Because it is not just democracy that has been broken—it is the purpose for which it exists, and the promises it made and lost. In the next chapter, we turn to that redemption—built on a foundation no longer rigged, corrupted, or hollow, but ready, once again, to serve the people.

7

PHASE IV: REDEMPTION — DELIVERING WHAT DEMOCRACY WAS MEANT TO PROVIDE

EIGHTEEN OUTCOMES THAT FULFILL THE CONSTITUTIONAL PROMISES

―――― ✦ ――――

"The test of our progress is not whether we add more to the abundance of those who have much; it is whether we provide enough for those who have too little." — Franklin D. Roosevelt

We do not rebuild a country by managing decline. We rebuild by daring to expect more—not just from our leaders, but from our democracy itself. The Restoration Agenda outlined in the last chapter makes the return of functional democracy possible. But functionality alone is not the goal. The American people were promised something greater: a nation that serves, protects, and lifts all of us. That promise has not been kept. The systems meant to deliver opportunity, care, fairness, and dignity have been broken or dismantled. Restoration is not ideology. It is the insistence that government work for the governed—and that freedom mean more than survival.

The Redemption Agenda is not an exhaustive blueprint. It does not replace legislation or settle debate. It defines outcomes: what a functional government, drawn from and answerable to the people, must make possible. These eighteen reforms are not about expanding the role of government for its own sake They are about expanding the power of the people to live with health, security, and dignity. Each paragraph offers a vision—what must be true in a restored republic if the constitutional promises are to mean something again. The how will vary. But the what is no longer negotiable.

I. A Nation That Cares for Its Own

Universal Health Care

A nation cannot be strong if its people are sick and afraid. Health care in America is a commodity, not a right—rationed by income, job status, and geography. Medical bankruptcies destroy lives. Families delay care or go without. Reform must guarantee access to essential care for every person, without financial ruin. Systems vary—single-payer, hybrid, public option—but the outcome must be universal, equitable, and protective. Preventive care should be prioritized. Mental health must be destigmatized. And no one should fear dying—or living—in debt. We already provide this to veterans. We must provide it to everyone. A healthy nation is not a luxury. It is a requirement of justice, stability, and resilience.

Affordable Housing

Shelter is not a privilege. It is the baseline for every other freedom. Yet in city after city, housing has become unattainable for working families. Rents soar. Mortgages exclude. Homelessness spreads. Zoning laws, speculation, and austerity policies all feed a system where profit is valued more than shelter. Reform must ensure that every person has access to safe, stable, affordable housing. This includes direct investment, tenant protections, anti-speculation measures, and incentives to build for need—not just wealth.

Housing policy is economic policy. It shapes where we live, how we work, what we earn, and how our children grow. A society that cannot house its people is not thriving. It is failing.

Food and Income Security

The richest nation on Earth has millions of children who go to school hungry. Food banks are overwhelmed. Wages stagnate while profits soar. The basic promise of a democracy—that those who work can live with dignity—is now broken. Redemption means rebuilding the safety net: secure nutrition programs, fair wages, and guaranteed minimum income where necessary. Unemployment insurance must reach the unemployed. Social programs must be easy to access, not designed for denial. And retirement should not mean poverty. A society where billionaires collect subsidies while children skip meals is not free. It is upside down. Real freedom begins when no one fears hunger or eviction.

Child Care and Family Support

No economy thrives when parents are forced to choose between work and care. And no society endures when its youngest citizens are treated as burdens, not investments. Today, child care is unaffordable, underpaid, and often unavailable—forcing millions, especially women, out of the workforce and deepening generational inequality. We must treat child care as essential infrastructure: publicly funded, professionally supported, and universally accessible. It means supporting parents through paid leave, flexible work, and family-based policies that strengthen—not strain—the bonds of care. A nation that cares for its own must begin with its children.

Fair Taxation and Wealth Reform

A nation's values are revealed by what it taxes and what it exempts. In America, wealth is protected while work is penalized. Billionaires pay lower effective rates than nurses and teachers. Corporations profit from public goods—roads, schools, research—without paying their share. A just tax system must restore fairness: progressive rates, wealth transparency, and the closing of loopholes that reward speculation. It means ensuring that those who benefit most from the system contribute most to its upkeep. A society cannot endure when the powerful hoard while the public crumbles. This is not punishment. It is patriotism. Democracy requires investment, and investment requires that the wealthiest among us pay what the nation needs to thrive.

II. A Nation That Educates and Elevates

Public Education Reform

Public education should be a ladder. Today, it is a lottery. Funding gaps, politicized curricula, crumbling infrastructure, and teacher shortages have left millions behind. Redemption means guaranteeing a high-quality education in every zip code—not just the wealthy ones. This requires equitable funding, universal pre-K, rigorous civics, and modernized classrooms. Teachers must be respected, supported, and paid. Curriculum must prepare students not for tests, but for life—as citizens, thinkers, workers, and leaders. The goal is not just economic mobility. It is democratic competence. An educated public is not a special interest. It is the foundation of every other right.

College Access and Debt Relief

Higher education is now a trap. Costs have exploded. Student debt tops $1.7 trillion. Degrees that once ensured stability now guarantee years of repayment. Reform must make public colleges affordable, student loans manageable, and technical training accessible. The goal is not just cancellation of past debts, but prevention of future ones. A college degree should open doors—not lock people into decades of financial constraint. In a knowledge economy, restricting education to the wealthy is not just unjust. It is self-defeating. We must unchain the next generation from a system that punishes learning and rewards exploitation.

Workforce and Labor Rights

Work is supposed to provide stability. For millions, it brings only exhaustion. Wages are stagnant. Benefits are slashed. Unions are attacked. Gig workers are excluded. We must restore the dignity of work: livable wages, safe conditions, collective bargaining rights, and predictable schedules. It means investing in training and transition programs so no worker is left behind in a changing economy. And it means ensuring that automation and globalization serve people—not just profits. A strong economy does not trickle down. It is built from the ground up—by workers who are treated as people, not costs to be minimized.

III. A Nation That Is Safe, Just, and Free

To Serve and Protect

Policing in America must be transformed from a tool of fear into a source of trust. Black Americans are disproportionately surveilled, arrested, and killed. Officers face few consequences. Communities feel abandoned or targeted—but rarely protected. Reform means accountability, transparency, de-escalation, and community investment. Federal support should depend on adherence to constitutional standards. The badge must not be a shield for abuse. And the justice system must treat all people equally—not based on their color, income, or ZIP code. Public safety begins when the public is safe—from crime and from the unchecked power of those sworn to prevent it.

Gun Policy Reform

America leads the world in gun deaths. Mass shootings traumatize communities. Routine violence destroys families. The leading cause of death in children is a bullet. And still, laws protect weapons more than people. The right to bear arms must be matched with the responsibility to protect life: background checks, safe storage, and common sense laws. Gun ownership should come with training, accountability, and enforcement. The Second Amendment cannot be a suicide pact. Freedom includes the freedom to live without fear in schools, churches, shopping centers, and homes. No parent should worry that sending a child to school might be a death sentence. This is not confiscation. It is common sense—and common decency.

Cybersecurity and Infrastructure Protection

Modern life depends on digital and physical infrastructure—from power grids to data networks, water systems to satellites. Yet these systems are vulnerable: to hackers, hostile states, and domestic sabotage. Cyberattacks can paralyze hospitals, elections, pipelines, and cities. Infrastructure neglect can end lives. Redemption means fortifying both the digital and physical veins of the republic. It means mandatory security standards, modernized systems, and a national strategy that prioritizes resilience over profit. Critical services must never rely on outdated code or crumbling pipes. Protecting infrastructure is not just technical. It is constitutional. A government that cannot defend its arteries cannot defend its people. Security is not just a budget line. It is the backbone of freedom.

Defending Democracy from Foreign Interference

No sovereign nation can survive if its decisions are made by outsiders. Yet America has tolerated foreign money in politics, foreign bots in discourse, and foreign blackmail in its highest offices. We must draw a bright line: no foreign donations, no shadow lobbying, no election manipulation disguised as free speech. It means transparency for campaign finance, digital ad verification, and airtight barriers between government and foreign interests. Defending democracy is not xenophobia. It is self-respect. A republic must be governed by its people—not by the ambitions of oligarchs, cartels, or hostile regimes. The next war may not come by invasion. It may come through silence, sabotage, and stolen sovereignty. We must be ready.

Criminal Justice Reform

Justice delayed is injustice sustained. America incarcerates more people than any other country—often for poverty-linked offenses. Sentencing is arbitrary. Bail locks up the poor before trial. Prisons are privatized, overcrowded, and underregulated. Reform means ending mandatory minimums, decriminalizing poverty, eliminating cash bail, and investing in rehabilitation over punishment. Police should not be the front line of mental health response. Prisons should not be warehouses for addiction and trauma. A fair justice system must recognize humanity—even in those who have committed harm. Accountability matters. So does restoration. A society that jails the poor and excuses the powerful is not just broken. It is backwards.

IV. A Nation That Belongs to Everyone

Immigration and Citizenship

Redemption means building a system that invites honesty, rewards contribution, and defends the dignity of belonging. America must offer more than punishment or panic. It must offer a lawful, accessible, and accountable path for those who come to live peacefully, work honestly, and contribute fully. We don't just need a wall. We need a door—and a standard. A path that welcomes those willing to walk it, and the courage to close it when trust is broken. This is not open borders. It is a functional contract—one that reflects our values without compromising safety or the rule of law.

Online Safety and Truth

Information is the bloodstream of democracy. Today, it is poisoned. Lies travel faster than facts. Platforms reward outrage. Foreign agents and domestic actors manipulate public opinion. Children face predation and bullying that can lead to self-harm and suicide. Adults face deception, division, and despair. Reform means transparent algorithms, verified political ads, enforceable content standards, and public oversight of digital spaces. Freedom of speech is not freedom to defraud. Regulation must protect both liberty and truth. We regulate food and drugs for safety. It is time to treat information the same way. The goal is not censorship. It is trust. A democracy that cannot tell truth from fiction will not survive.

Environmental Justice and Climate Action

The climate crisis is not future tense. It is now. Fires, floods, droughts, and storms kill Americans every year—disproportionately harming the poor and the powerless. Meanwhile, polluters profit, and action stalls. Redemption means rapid investment in clean energy, resilient infrastructure, and sustainable industry. It means holding corporations accountable and ensuring that frontline communities lead the transition. This is not just environmentalism. It is survival. We cannot rebuild a country on a dying planet. The future must be livable—for everyone, not just the wealthy. And the air we breathe and water we drink must be protected like the treasures they are.

V. This is the Redemption Agenda

It does not propose utopia. It proposes restoration. A nation that feeds its people. Heals its sick. Defends its rights. Rewards its work. Protects its planet. And upholds the dignity of all. These are not radical ideas. They are the reason governments exist. But no government dedicated to minority rule, no system rigged to serve only wealth and power, can fulfill these promises. First we restore democracy. Then we renew the nation to what it was designed to be.

This work will not be easy. Restoration changes structures. Redemption changes lives. It will take more than votes and legislation. It will take moral imagination and moral integrity. The discipline to think beyond self-interest. The humility to see others as fully human. The creativity to solve what others say is unsolvable. And the strength to keep going when cynicism and despair feel easier. We have done this before—after civil war, after economic collapse, after world war. We can do it again. We must do it again

And it will take leadership. Not just at the top, but at every level of government and civic life. The kind of courage that acts before it is safe and continues after it isn't. That endures exhaustion, ridicule, and even threat. That sees possibility in the void of resignation. It will take the kind of character, ethics, and integrity that inspire trust, awaken courage, and make others believe they can rise too—the kind that makes others say: *we can do this. We will do this.*

8

PHASE V: REINSTITUTION — THE RETURN TO RESTRAINT

THE FINAL TEST OF A SELF-GOVERNING PEOPLE

———◆———

"To govern is to choose, but to be free is to relinquish what you do not need." — JP Vincent

This phase of Reinstitution is our final chance to guarantee that democracy lasts another 250 years. If we reach this phase, it means we have survived the insurrection of 2021, the reelection of the Insurrectionist-in-Chief, and the attempted execution of Project 2025. It means we endured the hollowing of our courts, the sabotage of our elections, and the attempted concentration of all power in one man. It means we fought through collapse—and won. But winning is not the end. This final phase must ensure it cannot happen again. Then, and only then, can we step back and let democracy run without us holding it up.

Reinstitution is the quietest phase—but the most important. Defense held the line. Resistance exposed the regime. Restoration seized the tools. Redemption proved the system could serve again. Reinstitution must now take what was seized and put it back—

corrected, refined, and restrained. This is not restoration of the old. It is the establishment of a new democratic baseline: built from experience, scarred by collapse, and unwilling to gamble with freedom again. Every empire that has ever survived learned this truth too late: that strength is not shown in how long you hold power, but in how deliberately you let it go.

The greatest threat in this final phase is not defeat, but success without restraint. History is replete with revolutions that won justice and lost legitimacy. Power, even when righteously won, carries the same risks it always did: inertia, arrogance, abuse. Reinstitution is the only phase that asks nothing for itself. It is the final measure of democratic maturity. No court order will force it. No political reward will follow it. But if we do not do it, everything we rebuilt will be seen not as restoration, but as replacement. Not as fairness, but as revenge. Not as democracy, but as capture.

This is the moment to remember the precedent of Washington: the general who could have ruled for life, but stepped down. Or Lincoln, who insisted on elections in the middle of a civil war. Or the architects of the Marshall Plan, who chose to rebuild former enemies instead of exploiting them. In each case, the greatest act of power was restraint. The refusal to dominate. The deliberate return of tools, lands, or laws that could have been used to entrench advantage. Reinstitution is our generation's test of this principle. It is how we show the world we deserve to endure.

This will not be easy. We are emerging from an era in which power was hoarded, rules were broken, and every branch of government was warped toward personal gain. Project 2025 sought not just dominance but permanence. Undoing that will require extraordinary reforms. But making those reforms last requires something harder still: self-restraint in victory. The forces that broke the republic will not vanish. They will regroup, rebrand, and wait. We must make the new rules strong enough to stop them—but fair enough to bind us, too. If we cheat better, we do not win. We merely delay collapse.

The temptation to hold extraordinary tools indefinitely is not a flaw—it is a feature of power itself. But democracy depends on the refusal of that temptation. Reinstitution is the recognition that the means of emergency governance are not the means of self-rule. Expand the Court to unrig it—but return it to balance. End the filibuster to pass democracy's rescue—but replace it with deliberation, not silence. Reclaim executive authority to rebuild—but then bind it with law. We must act decisively to fix what was broken. But then, with equal clarity, choose to step back from the edge.

Reinstitution is not repeal. Not every reform needs to be undone. Some tools were overdue. Some powers were wrongly denied. What we keep must be justified—clearly, publicly, and permanently. But what we return must be meaningful, too. Restraint is not weakness. It is signal. A republic that cannot let go of power cannot last. We must make the case for permanence carefully: What safeguards are now essential? What checks must never again be optional? What powers must always be divided, never hoarded? The answers must be institutional, cultural, and constitutional. Law alone will not hold the line.

Some reforms must be made permanent through constitutional amendment. These include: an explicit federal right to vote, enforced judicial ethics, term limits for Supreme Court justices, the end of absolute immunity for presidents, and the permanent ban on partisan gerrymandering. These are not party victories. They are structural guarantees. But each comes with a cost: time, unity, and discipline. Reinstitution must not abandon ambition—it must finish the work of Resistance, Restoration and Redemption. But it must finish it with honesty. We cannot lock in what benefits us and call it fairness. We must lock in what protects everyone.

There is a category of emergency tools that must not remain:

expanded courts, temporary appointments, expedited authority powers, extraordinary prosecutorial reach, emergency communication laws. These served their purpose. But left unchecked, they become indistinguishable from authoritarian tools. Reinstitution means sunsetting them—through law, not habit. Their expiration must be written in statute. Their return must require supermajority consent. They cannot be wielded again casually, by those who did not see why they were created. If we do not bind ourselves, we will be bound by fear again. Democracy must learn to live without the crutches that saved it.

This phase also requires something less tangible, but no less urgent: a reformation of civic memory. Americans must remember what happened. The trials. The lies. The lawsuits. The rallies. The pardons. The purges. The slow violence of law manipulated and freedom undermined. Reinstitution is where the story is written—not just in lawbooks, but in schoolbooks, museums, public media, and shared rituals. We must make the truth undeniable and unshakable. Because if memory fades, tyranny returns. And if future generations are taught that fairness was a weapon, not a shield, then all our restraint will look like defeat.

Trust must become a structural goal. Not a political asset. Not a communications tactic. A goal. It must be measurable, visible, and pursued like the economy or national security. Reinstitution means embedding public legitimacy into the architecture of government itself. Transparent budgeting. Automatic public oversight. Real-time data on service delivery. Justice that is seen, not just done. Trust cannot be assumed. It must be earned anew, and then protected as its own kind of infrastructure. Because when trust erodes, power fills the vacuum. Reinstitution is what prevents that cycle from beginning again.

This is the time to codify new democratic norms. Every appointment process must be public, accountable, and time-bound. Redistricting must produce maps where a state's delegation reflects the political makeup of its voters. Every branch of government must operate under a codified ethical code enforceable by law. These are not future dreams. They are urgent necessities. Reinstitution is not a delay. It is the most important construction phase of all—because it makes what we rebuilt resistant to collapse. If we do not embed these norms into statute, precedent, and culture, they will be undone in the next season of apathy or rage.

Guardrails must not just restrain enemies. They must bind allies. That is the moral difference between authoritarian and democratic power. Authoritarians build for advantage. Democracies build for durability. Reinstitution is how we demonstrate that distinction—by building systems that prevent even our own excesses. Because we will be tempted. We will be impatient. We will be attacked. And if we build for ourselves, we will fail. But if we build for a republic that outlasts us, then this moment will matter beyond us. That is the difference between control and citizenship. Between possession and service.

Emergency powers must come with built-in expiration. Every grant of extraordinary authority—economic, judicial, military, communicative—must include a timeline, a review process, and an oversight body. And no emergency power should continue without explicit reauthorization. Congress must ratify any presidential request to extend or renew these powers. Never again can one man with a Sharpie declare an economic emergency, invoke the Alien Enemies Act, or claim a border invasion alone. The United States still holds hundreds of dormant statutes enabling sweeping control over markets, movement, speech, and dissent. Reinstitution must review, revise, or repeal them. Because no democracy survives emergency without end—and no free people should ever live beneath one.

We must also reimagine what humility looks like in government. Reinstitution is where we voluntarily step down, rotate leadership, defer to others, and decentralize power—but never abandon responsibility. The federal government must remain strong enough to enforce rights, ensure fairness, and protect truth. Let governors lead more. Let local councils decide more. But only within national standards that prevent the return of injustice. The goal is not to let states do as they please, but to let people see their will enacted close to home—without fear of erasure. True restraint is not retreat. It is structured trust, under law. That is the real strength of humility.

Reinstitution sends a message beyond our borders: that the American experiment did not just survive—it matured. That we did not simply remove a tyrant, but removed the tools that made tyranny possible. In a century of rising autocracy, that is not a small signal. It is a beacon. And it will echo further than any speech or summit. If we finish this work, we will have shown the world that democracy is not naïve, not weak, not outdated—but resilient, self-correcting, and worthy of imitation. And even, when standing on the brink of self-destruction, can come back. Stronger.

The reforms we secure during Reinstitution are not just for us. They are for a generation that has not yet voted, marched, or governed. They will inherit what we institutionalize. If we institutionalize fear, they will govern with suspicion. If we institutionalize fairness, they will govern with pride. Reinstitution must be designed not just for the present crisis, but for the next century of self-government. And the one after that. If we do this right, our children and their great-grandchildren will not need to repeat this cycle. They will defend democracy not from ruins, but from strength.

We must begin this phase neither too early nor too late. Too early, and we risk unraveling what we just built. Too late, and we risk never letting go. Reinstitution requires discipline, timing, and clarity. We must know what to sunset and when. We must pass reform packages with built-in triggers. We must monitor public sentiment without being ruled by it. This is the least glamorous phase. But it is the most revealing. It shows who we are when we are not in crisis. It shows whether we built a system—or just seized a moment.

The paradox of power is that the only ones worthy of it are those willing to give it up. Reinstitution is the final act of leadership. It is not the seizing of control, but the return to balance. We end this plan not by locking the gates, but by opening them wider. Not by asserting dominance, but by guaranteeing dignity. We do not do this because we are naïve. We do it because we are ready. And because we remember what happened when the tools of democracy were used to destroy it. That cannot be allowed again.

This is the final test. Not of resistance. Not of intelligence. But of restraint. If we pass it, democracy becomes self-sustaining again—guided not by vengeance, but by vision. If we fail, we may become what we once opposed. The hardest thing to do with power is not to wield it well—but to walk away from it when it is no longer needed. This is that moment. If we build the right system, it will not need us anymore. And that will be the truest proof we ever had—that the Constitution still lives, not just on paper, but in practice. And that the republic still stands—because we refused to let it fall.

9

THE RESPONSIBILITY OF POWER
EMERGENCY POWERS, ETHICAL FAILURE, AND THE LONG ROAD BACK

"The only argument for self-government that endures: it must work, and it must work for all." — JP Vincent

The Constitution does not act. The courts do not rise. The vote does not count itself. Only people can do that. And after all the plans, after all the reforms, after all the restoration—what remains is this: democracy is not what we write. It is what we do. This is not a sixth phase. It is the moment after the plan, when the burden shifts. From policy to person. From institution to will. From what we rebuilt, to how we carry it. And whether it lasts.

Trump did not break the system. He revealed how broken it already was. Voting rights had been gutted one court ruling at a time. Wages stagnated while corporate profits soared. Public schools in poor districts crumbled while billionaires launched vanity rockets. Homelessness rose not from crisis, but from policy. The gap between the rich and the merely stable widened year after year.

Healthcare became a luxury. Incarceration became a business model. These weren't signs of sudden collapse—they were symptoms of a long decay. And through it all, democracy was weakened not by force, but by erosion. Not by a dictator's command, but by the quiet shrug of a nation too tired to care.

Then Trump came—not as the cause of collapse, but as its confirmation. In just over a hundred days, he fired watchdogs, defied court rulings, defunded agencies, and rewrote rules. He pardoned violent extremists, installed incompetent loyalists, profited off cryptocurrency, sold access to donors, withheld aid from disloyal states, and silenced dissent using the machinery of government. All with a one-dollar Sharpie. He seized power not with violence, but with a pen—because nothing stood in his way. But no vibrant democracy can be overturned with a signature. No functioning republic allows immunity to be granted like favor, or agencies dissolved on a whim, or tens of thousands purged in a fit of personal revenge. If power can be bought—or grabbed with a signature—if justice can be ignored, if oversight can be fired, then what we had was not protection—it was performance. A shell painted in patriotic words, hollowed out by decades of corruption and retreat.

We were told this was normal. That money was speech, that influence was just access, that patronage was a feature, not a flaw. But when billionaires become secretaries, when lobbyists write the bills, when think tanks write the governing playbook, what we have is not democracy. What we have is capture. It has happened in autocracies before—and it is happening now, here, in the open, without apology.

The Supreme Court cloaked itself in robes and ritual, but even sanctity has limits. When Justices accept lavish vacations from billionaires with cases before them, refuse to recuse, fly partisan flags from their homes, and issue rulings that defy the plain reading of law, the myth collapses. The Court is no longer a temple of law. It is a battlefield of ideology—a shield for the few, and the one. The law has become political. And a weapon. And targeted political law is no law at all.

We have seen them grant immunity where none should exist, delay justice until it no longer matters, and reverse decades of settled precedent in the service of a movement—not a nation. These are not the errors of wise men. These are the decisions of power brokers cloaked in marble. A court that rules to protect the ruler is no check on tyranny—it is its enabler. And no democracy can survive a captured court.

But the tools used to break democracy can also rebuild it. Trump proved how powerful emergency authority can be. He used it to punish critics, manipulate markets, rewrite maps, and silence the civil service. He redirected billions without appropriation, erased protections by fiat, and claimed new powers simply by asserting them. If such power exists—and clearly it does—it can be wielded not just to destroy, but to restore.

Emergency authority has been used to deport citizens to foreign prisons, suppress scientific findings, and reward allies with public funds. But those same tools can be used to secure fair elections, expand healthcare, stabilize the climate, and rebuild trust in public institutions. What is dangerous in the hands of the lawless is essential in the hands of those who govern with integrity. We do not need new tools—we need new intent. The power already exists. It must now be reclaimed.

This is not about revenge. It is about responsibility. The power that was abused must not be discarded—it must be re-anchored in law, constrained by justice, and directed toward restoration. We must use that power to build the systems that were torn down, to protect those who were cast aside, and to ensure that no future demagogue can wield it without restraint. Then, and only then, can it be dismantled.

Because restoration is not enough. A repaired machine can still serve injustice. We need more than elections. We need results. The eighteen Redemption initiatives are not idealism. They are necessity. A system that functions only to keep the wealthy secure and the poor struggling is not worth preserving. A democracy must be judged not by the elegance of its constitution, but by the conditions of its people. And ours are unacceptable.

People will not choose democracy if democracy does not choose them. If they are hungry, homeless, sick, or hopeless, they will choose fear. And fear always finds a candidate. If we want democracy to survive, it must deliver. Not in speeches. Not in symbols. But in lives saved, children fed, jobs created, rights protected. That is the only argument for self-government that endures: it must work, and it must work for all.

Once it does, the emergency must end. Power that is unbound, even in the service of justice, becomes a threat. The goal is not permanent control—it is permanent fairness. Once oversight is restored, elections secured, and trust rebuilt, the powers used to protect democracy must be locked away. What we wield in crisis must not become custom. There must be a clear end. Otherwise, the new order becomes the old danger, reborn.

It will be tempting to hold on—to say "just a little longer." But every autocracy in history has said the same. Every movement has believed it could manage exceptional power indefinitely. It cannot. We do not need a new ruler. We need a new republic. And that means knowing when to stop. Knowing when the tools have served their purpose. And knowing that democracy, to live, must breathe.

This will take extraordinary people. Not heroes. Not saviors. But ordinary citizens with extraordinary will. Judges who remember that law is a duty, not a weapon. Journalists who speak truth even when no one listens. Bureaucrats who do their job in silence, with integrity. Teachers who light minds in systems that try to darken them. Voters who keep showing up, even when the system tries to turn them away.

It will take lawyers who value justice more than victory. Legislators who care more about their oath than their seat. Scientists who defend fact. Activists who outlast despair. And donors—yes, donors—who finally understand that their privilege was bought with the wreckage of a nation. They must help rebuild it. Not with slogans, but with sacrifice. Not with lobbying, but with humility. The time for neutrality is over.

This is not a call to idealism. It is a call to duty. The restoration of democracy requires labor—tedious, thankless, daily labor. It will not happen in a single election. It will not be won with a single speech. It will take years. It will take patience. And it will take a refusal to forget what was done, what was lost, and what we owe to those who are not yet born.

So who will do it? Who will rise not to save the nation, but to serve it? Who will stand not for applause, but for principle? There will be no announcement. No endorsement. No rescue from above. There is only the moment—and the decision to show up. To take responsibility. To begin again, even when beginning feels impossible. To carry a torch through the dark, not because you know the way, but because someone has to.

There is no other generation. There is no other time. If democracy is to rise, it must rise from us. We are the ones here. We are the ones alive. No one is coming who is better prepared, more committed, smarter, more principled, or has more to lose. If we still believe in liberty, in justice, in decency, then we must be the ones who act.

And without permission. Without hesitation. With unity, courage, and growing fire. Until the work is done.

APPENDIX A: THE RESTORATION AGENDA: 18 STRUCTURAL REFORMS TO REBUILD A FAIR DEMOCRACY

"Power must be made visible before it can be held accountable." — JP Vincent

These eighteen reforms form the foundation of The American Restoration. They are not designed to tilt the system toward any party, but to restore what democracy requires: fair elections, coequal branches, legal accountability, and public trust. Each reform addresses a structural failure that has already been exploited. Together, they offer a blueprint to rebuild a republic in which power flows from the people—not from donors, courts, or kings.

I. Elections That Count Every Voice

1. **Campaign Finance Reform:** Overturn *Citizens United* and end dark money; mandate full donor transparency; create public financing options.
2. **Voting Rights Protection:** Reinstate and modernize the

Voting Rights Act; restore preclearance; standardize early/mail voting and access.
3. **Electoral College Reform:** Complete the National Popular Vote Compact and harden federal safeguards against elector substitution schemes.
4. **Redistricting Reform:** Require all states to use independent commissions with fairness metrics to draw electoral districts.
5. **Election Certification Integrity:** Federally protect election officials, block false elector slates, and lock in secure certification processes.

II. Checks on Presidential Power

6. **Presidential Accountability:** Legislate that presidents are not immune from prosecution for personal, criminal, or unconstitutional acts.
7. **Oversight Independence and Protection:** Establish statutory protections for Inspectors General, strengthen whistleblower safeguards, and enforce compliance with Congressional oversight.
8. **Emergency Powers Reform:** Require automatic expiration and congressional review for national emergencies; limit unilateral power grabs.
9. **Executive Order Oversight:** Require congressional review for executive orders affecting constitutional rights or federal spending.
10. **Pardon Power Constraints:** Prohibit self-pardons and secret pardons; require public reporting and DOJ review of all clemency.

III. A Judiciary That Upholds Law, Not Loyalty

11. **Supreme Court Term Limits:** Enact fixed term limits for justices to depoliticize judicial timing and restore generational balance.
12. **Lower Court Expansion:** Add judges to handle backlog and reduce ideological capture through deliberate neglect.
13. **Supreme Court Ethics Code:** Enforce binding standards on gifts, recusals, financial disclosure, and conflict of interest.
14. **Insurrection Clause Enforcement:** Operationalize Section 3 of the 14th Amendment to disqualify public officials engaged in rebellion.
15. **Transparency and FOIA Modernization:** Shorten timelines, narrow exemptions, and apply open-government standards to privatized public functions.

IV. Rebuilding an Informed Public

16. **Disinformation and Platform Transparency:** Require disclosure of political ad sources; implement civic audits for algorithmic manipulation during elections.
17. **Fairness in Broadcast Media:** Enact a modernized Fairness Doctrine to require balanced coverage in publicly licensed broadcasting.
18. **Civic Education and Democratic Literacy:** Fund universal civics instruction; support national service and democratic engagement training.

APPENDIX B: THE REDEMPTION AGENDA – FIXING WHAT NO LONGER WORKS

"Democracy is not just the right to vote. It is the right to live in dignity." — Naomi Klein

These eighteen reforms define the Redemption Agenda—the second phase of *American Renewal: A Manifesto for Resistance, a Blueprint for Restoration, and a Vision for Redemption*. They are not theories or aspirations. They are democratic requirements. Each one sets a clear outcome that a just and functional government must be able to deliver—across health, housing, education, labor, safety, climate, and shared belonging. These reforms are not grouped by bureaucracy but by promise: what a free nation must guarantee its people. They are not the final destination. But without them, no country can claim to be free, fair, or whole.

I. A Nation That Cares for Its Own

1. **Universal Health Care:** Guarantee access to essential

health services for all people, without financial ruin, delay, or discrimination.
2. **Affordable Housing:** Ensure access to safe, stable, and affordable shelter in every community, with protections against speculation and displacement.
3. **Food and Income Security:** Eliminate hunger and poverty through nutrition programs, fair wages, unemployment access, and secure retirement.
4. **Child Care and Family Support:** Treat child care as essential infrastructure by funding universal access, raising wages, and supporting parents through paid leave, flexible work, and family-based policies.
5. **Fair Taxation and Wealth Reform:** Restore fairness to the tax code through progressive rates, wealth transparency, and the elimination of loopholes that reward speculation over contribution.

II. A Nation That Educates and Elevates

6. **Public Education Reform:** Deliver high-quality public education in every zip code, supported by equitable funding and professional respect for teachers.
7. **College Access and Debt Relief:** Make public higher education affordable, student debt manageable, and technical training universally accessible.
8. **Workforce and Labor Rights:** Protect the dignity of work with livable wages, benefits, safety, and rights for all workers, including the gig economy.

III. A Nation That Is Safe, Just, and Free

9. **To Serve and Protect:** Reform policing and public safety to ensure accountability, de-escalation, and equal justice under law.
10. **Gun Policy Reform:** Reduce gun violence through background checks, assault weapon restrictions, and safety laws that prioritize life.
11. **Cybersecurity and Infrastructure Protection:** Establish national standards to secure digital and physical infrastructure—from elections to energy grids—against cyberattacks, sabotage, and systemic neglect.
12. **Defending Democracy from Foreign Interference:** Ban foreign donations, shadow lobbying, and digital manipulation to ensure elections are decided by the people, not by hostile regimes or outside influence.
13. **Criminal Justice Reform:** Eliminate cash bail, end mass incarceration, and invest in rehabilitation over punishment.

IV. A Nation That Belongs to Everyone

14. **Immigration and Citizenship:** Replace cruelty and chaos with a fair, humane, and efficient system rooted in due process and human dignity.
15. **Online Safety and Truth:** Regulate digital platforms to defend against disinformation, manipulation, and online harm.
16. **Environmental Justice and Climate Action:** Combat the climate crisis through rapid, equitable investment in clean energy and community resilience.

V. A Nation That Prepares for the Future

17. **Digital Infrastructure and Access Equity:** Guarantee universal broadband access and treat digital connection as a public good.
18. **Public Service and Civic Reengagement:** Expand national service and civic education programs to renew democratic participation and shared purpose.

APPENDIX C: HOW TO BE READY WHEN THE KNOCK COMES

"We don't rise to the level of our hopes. We fall to the level of our preparation." — Archilochus

Someone you know may be taken. Not charged. Not tried. Just—taken. A student, a neighbor, a co-worker, someone from your church. In an era of lawless power, people disappear not because they are guilty, but because they are vulnerable. And whether they are released or vanish depends on how quickly—and how visibly—others respond. In one town, it was a mother and her children. In another, a graduate student. In both cases, people acted before the silence could settle. That's what saved them. Not the system. The response. And response only happens if you're ready. This is not alarmism. It's discipline—the kind that keeps people from disappearing. The kind that turns neighbors into defenders.

These we prepare to defend:

- A student who shared the wrong post.
- A teacher who taught the wrong book.

- A journalist who published truth the government calls treason.
- A doctor who offered reproductive care.
- A trans kid trying to survive.
- A pastor offering shelter.
- A protester with a sign.
- A neighbor with a name that sounds foreign.
- A person with no papers but decades of contribution.
- A stranger who deserves not to be disappeared.

These are not hypotheticals. These are people already taken—detained in rural ICE facilities, questioned by federal agents over tweets, blacklisted from naturalization, held without charges. What protected them was not innocence—it was response. What failed others was not the law, but the absence of anyone to call, anyone to act, anyone to watch. The government's goal is not always conviction. Often, it is disappearance: temporary, indefinite, invisible. The opposite of disappearance is preparation. It means knowing what to do before the moment strikes. It means having a plan, not just an instinct.

If You Believe You May Be a Target

Legal Preparation

- Retain counsel. For immigrants, both immigration and criminal defense.
- Prepare a packet: ID, legal documents, medical needs, power of attorney, emergency contacts.
- Photograph everything. Store securely. Give copies to a trusted friend or lawyer—**someone who doesn't live with you**.
- Carry a Know Your Rights card in your wallet at all times.

Communication Protocol

- Set up a Signal group that includes: your legal contact, someone who can go public fast, and someone who will stay private.
- Share your live location with someone at all times.
- Assign one lead contact to activate your response plan instantly.

Documentation and Oversight

- Back up all sensitive data to secure, remote platforms—encrypted and out of reach.
- Use apps that auto-upload photos, audio, and video the moment they're taken.
- **Practice the first 30 seconds**—not just once, but until you can do it half-asleep.

You won't have time to think.

You'll have time to act—if you've practiced. The knock, the shout, the flashing lights, the sudden grip on your arm in a store aisle—every form of intimidation is meant to short-circuit your response. Scare you. Confuse you. Leave you immobile. You must train for it now, in your own home, with the people around you. You may have only 30 seconds. Seconds that may make the difference between freedom and disappearance.

What to say (if private):

- "I do not consent to a search."
- "I am exercising my right to remain silent."
- "I want to speak to a lawyer."

Say nothing else.

What to say (if public):

- Say loudly: "I do not consent!"
- Shout your full name.
- Next: "Record this! Record this!"
- If you know you're being recorded, shout clearly: "Call [your practiced contact's name]!"
- Then repeat—for as long as you can.

What to do:

- Never open the door without a signed warrant. Ask to see it through a window or peephole.
- If they force their way in, stay calm. Do not resist. Do not assist.
- Immediately notify your emergency contact or Signal group.
- Turn on your phone's audio recorder as soon as you hear the knock. Put your phone in your pocket—don't keep it in your hand if you don't have to.
- Practice now with your household: who films, who calls, who documents.
- Set your phone so all media auto-uploads to the cloud.
- Teach others how to retrieve those backups if your phone is taken.

Survival is not luck. It is preparation.

If Someone Else Is Taken

Recognize the Signs

- Disappearance. Missed class or work. A silent phone. A rumor of a raid.
- Always ask. Always check. You may be the first to notice something's wrong.

Document Everything

- Film the moment it happens. Even one photo may help.
- Record: license plates, timestamps, agent names, locations, and badge numbers.
- Use apps that upload instantly. **Label what you capture: date, time, place, identities, if safe.**
- **Listen for the person's name—and remember it. Listen for the name they shout to call—and call them.**

Form Your Signal Group Now

- Include: civil rights lawyers, immigration advocates, reporters, local TV/radio, elected officials, university clinics, public defenders, and clergy.
- Assign backup admins who can remove members, delete the group, or rename it if someone is compromised.
- Plan for visibility—but also know when invisibility protects.

Mobilize in Minutes or Hours, Not Days

- Organize a rally, call-in, or media push within 24 hours.

- Pre-write a public statement. Assign a spokesperson. Track the detainee.
- Choose a gathering point where people can meet, film, and be seen.

Push for Legal Relief and Public Pressure

- Demand a bond hearing. Prevent transfer. Keep the case local.
- Involve state officials. Make sure media is watching.
- The system rarely responds to morality. It responds to visibility.

This Is Civic Discipline

Every school, workplace, church, family, and community group should walk through these steps—not to frighten, but to be ready. Not every arrest can be stopped, but every disappearance can be resisted. If you are silent, they vanish. If you are prepared, they may come home. The knock is coming—for someone. The only question is whether you'll be ready when it does. We do not prepare because we believe the law will save us. We prepare because silence won't. And we do not prepare out of fear. We prepare because readiness is the beginning of resistance.

APPENDIX D: PERSONAL READINESS – LEGAL, DIGITAL, AND EMERGENCY PREPARATION

"You prepare not because you expect to be taken. You prepare because you refuse to let others be taken alone." — JP Vincent

Preparation is not one-size-fits-all. What follows is not a script—it is a guide. Some steps may not apply to you. Others may apply to someone you love, someone you live with, or someone you're responsible for. Take what you need. Adapt what you must. The goal is not perfection—it is readiness. These checklists are not about fear. They are about control, clarity, and care. They are about making sure that when something happens, you are not frozen. You are not scattered. You are not alone. In this chapter, readiness is defined not by escape, but by resistance: the kind that holds space, buys time, and refuses to vanish. Quietly, steadily, we prepare.

Section I. Legal Readiness

The law may not save you—but preparation can buy time, create leverage, and keep your disappearance from becoming permanent. Legal readiness means ensuring someone can prove who you are, what rights you hold, and who should be called the moment you're taken. It means ensuring your legal presence can outlive your physical absence. This is not paranoia—it is strategic foresight. The system rarely protects those it targets, but it sometimes responds to pressure. For that pressure to be applied quickly, someone must already have what they need. That is what this section ensures: not just your safety, but your reappearance. Quietly assembling these documents and contacts is one of the most radical acts of solidarity you can perform—for yourself or anyone you love.

What to do:

- Retain a lawyer now, or know exactly who you'll call if targeted
- Carry a Know Your Rights card in your wallet
- Prepare a legal packet:
    - Government-issued ID
    - Passport, birth certificate, immigration records
    - Medical information and prescriptions
    - Power of attorney, guardianship papers if applicable
- Photograph every document and back it up to the cloud
- Share full copies with a trusted friend or attorney who does **not** live with you

Section II. Digital Readiness

In the wrong hands, your phone becomes a weapon—not just against you, but against everyone you've spoken to, filmed, or supported. Digital readiness is about protection, not erasure. You don't need to live in hiding—but you must take seriously the risks of carrying unprotected data. Your photos, messages, contacts, and locations can all be accessed if your phone is taken. The goal is not to make yourself invisible. The goal is to make it impossible to silence you by stealing your device. Digital preparation ensures that what you know survives, what you've seen is uploaded, and who you've protected stays protected. This is how you guard the truth, your networks, and the record.

What to do:

- Back up all sensitive files to secure, encrypted cloud storage
- Use strong passwords and 2-factor authentication on every key account
- Enable remote wipe on all devices
- Clear your device of anything you cannot protect
- Share passwords with one trusted person via a secure password manager
- Turn on automatic upload for all media: photos, videos, and audio
- Practice accessing your backups from a second device

Section III. Communication Readiness

Your voice doesn't need to go silent just because you're gone. Communication readiness is the art of ensuring others know what to do if you disappear. That begins with a Signal group, continues with public instructions, and ends with a network that does not need your permission to act. Your communication plan is not just about alerting your closest contacts. It's about triggering a response —a statement, a search, a strategy—before silence settles in. Build your team now. Choose your public voice now. Decide what should be said about you while you cannot speak. A fast, coordinated response is not built in the moment. It is built before it's needed.

What to do:

- Create a Signal group or other encrypted chat for emergencies
- Include legal contacts, a public voice, and someone who will stay private
- Assign at least two other group admins who can rename, delete, or secure the group if you're detained
- Share your live location with someone at all times
- Establish a check-in rhythm: if you go dark for 12 hours, who acts?
- Write a short public statement now for others to release if you're taken
- Make your wishes clear: do you want them to go public? Stay quiet? Who should speak for you?

Section IV. Emergency Readiness

They will not wait. So you cannot either. If you are forced to flee, hide, or turn yourself in, you may have only minutes. Emergency readiness is not about assuming the worst. It's about denying panic the upper hand. You prepare now so that everything you need is in one place, and everyone you trust knows where to find it. A go-bag is not just about escape—it's about continuity. It is how you care for dependents, retrieve your records, and rebuild your contact with the world if your devices are lost or your home is searched. Emergency readiness is an act of calm defiance. It says: *You may disrupt my life, but you will not destroy it.*

What to do:

- Prepare a go-bag with:
    - Copies of all legal and medical documents
    - Medications
    - Backup phone

- o Prepaid debit card
  - o House keys and any critical items
- Write down key contacts in case your phone is lost
- Make a plan for children, pets, or others who depend on you
- Identify local legal clinics, ACLU chapters, and elected officials you can contact in an emergency
- Print hard copies of everything in case digital access fails

Section V. Outreach and Escalation Resources

Preparedness doesn't end with your own readiness. It extends to who you can activate, how fast you can escalate, and where the truth will land. This section is about making power and press contactable. When someone disappears, speed and scale are everything. That means knowing in advance who you'll call, who will publish the story, and which office will hear your demand. Save these contacts now. Store them offline. Share them with others. This is how you shorten the gap between silence and spotlight. The state moves quickly. So must we.

Find and save now:

- Your U.S. Representative and Senator (look them up at the official House and Senate websites)
- Your state Attorney General (search the National Association of Attorneys General)
- Your local officials (BallotReady or your county's elections office)
- Your nearest ACLU affiliate (listed at aclu.org)
- Local Legal Aid offices (search via the Legal Services Corporation)

- Names, numbers, and emails of journalists, TV, and radio outlets
- Civil rights organizations—both local and national
- Trusted upload platforms: YouTube, TikTok, Twitter/X, Instagram, Signal, SecureDrop
- A backup folder for fast broadcasting: timeline, photos, names, documents, and a public statement

Section VI. What to Record If You Witness a Raid or Abduction

When they come, they count on confusion. On no one noticing. On fear. You break that by recording, remembering, and repeating what you saw. When someone is taken, your job is not just to witness—it is to preserve proof and name the act. Do not intervene unless you must. But do not look away. Film. Speak the time and place aloud. Say the name of the person being taken. Watch what's said, what's done, and what disappears. Your footage may be the only truth that survives. Record like someone's freedom depends on it—because it may.

What to film:

- License plates, agent names, badges, vehicles
- What they say: "we have a warrant," "you're being detained," "you're under arrest"
- Who they take: name, clothing, bags, children
- What they take: phones, IDs, documents
- Time, date, and place—say it aloud on camera
- Repeat the person's name and the name they shout to call
- Film continuously, upload immediately, and get the footage off your phone fast

Section VII. This Is Solidarity in Action

You are not preparing because you expect to be taken. You are preparing because someone might—and they must not face it alone. These checklists are not defensive. They are defiant. They refuse silence. They refuse shame. They refuse the machinery of erasure. When you prepare like this, you become part of a quiet, distributed network that makes vanishing harder and justice louder. You cannot stop them from knocking. But you can make sure the knock echoes. You can ensure it is seen, heard, recorded, reported, and resisted. This is what it means to be ready. This is how we hold the line.

READER'S GUIDES
REFLECTIONS, ACTIONS, AND STRATEGIC QUESTIONS FOR EVERY CHAPTER

---◆---

These Reader's Guides are not summaries. They are tools—for reflection, discussion, and action. Each guide corresponds to a chapter in *American Renewal*, offering structure to help readers engage more deeply with the material. Their purpose is not to repeat the argument, but to extend it—to ask what it demands of us now.

Each guide begins by framing the stakes and summarizing the structural failure at hand. It then offers a list of action-focused imperatives, a strategic rationale for the reform, and practical suggestions for what individual readers can do. Finally, each ends with a set of discussion questions—designed for classrooms, book clubs, community forums, or solitary thought.

The goal is simple: to turn understanding into momentum, and insight into repair. Democracy does not rebuild itself. It takes people —alert, informed, and willing to act. These guides were written to help.

Reader's Guide: Chapter 1—The Collapse Of The Constitutional Promise

The Stakes

The Constitution does not promise comfort. It promises constraint. It is not a license for government power—it is a restriction on it. But that restriction only holds if the people recognize when it is being broken. The first hundred days of Trump's second term have revealed what it means to govern without guardrails. Justice is discretionary. Speech is chilled. Law is wielded like a weapon. This is not erosion. It is collapse. And unless it is reversed, the United States will continue drifting into constitutional fiction—where institutions remain but no longer serve.

THE STRUCTURE

This chapter is not a historical overview. It is a record of six failures, each corresponding to one of the Constitution's foundational promises: union, justice, tranquility, defense, welfare, and liberty. Each section of the chapter matches one of these constitutional charges, not as abstractions but as functions of governance. The promise of a republic is evaluated not by sentiment or symbolism, but by performance. By that measure, every founding duty has been betrayed—and not accidentally, but deliberately, in service of concentrated power and unchecked rule.

THE COLLAPSE

What once constrained power now enables it. The courts no longer protect rights—they rewrite limits to suit their own. The Department of Justice prosecutes protestors, not the president.

Public servants are purged and replaced with sycophants. Emergency powers are invoked not to save the nation, but to bypass its laws. Elections are manipulated by design. Surveillance is normalized. The union fractures into weaponized factions, and justice bends toward loyalty. These are not warning signs. They are symptoms of a system that is failing on purpose.

The Remedy

Reversing collapse begins with refusal. Refusal to normalize the chaos, accept the propaganda, or treat systemic failure as individual fault. The constitutional order must be rebuilt—not nostalgically, but structurally. The reforms that follow in this book are not wish lists or white papers. They are restorations of function: how to reintroduce constraint where impunity reigns, and how to create institutions that serve public interest rather than private command. There is no singular fix. But there is a path. And that path begins with truth plainly spoken: the system is broken, and those breaking it must be removed from power.

What Comes Next

This chapter ends with collapse. The next one begins with confrontation. It defines, step by step, how the six constitutional promises—union, justice, tranquility, defense, welfare, and liberty—can be restored. Not rhetorically, but operationally. Each promise is treated as a measurable outcome of governance. Together, they will form the blueprint for restoration. Then the final chapter of Volume 1 begins to build what comes after: a democracy that works. Not in theory. In law, in practice, and in trust.

Three Things to Remember

- The Constitution defines government's duties—and each one is now broken.
- Collapse is not accidental. It is the intended outcome of power without constraint.
- Restoration requires structural reform, not just better leadership.

Action List

- Confront the collapse: name it, prove it, refuse to normalize it.
- Document what's broken: union, justice, tranquility, defense, welfare, liberty.
- Expose the architects: who benefits, who enables, who must be removed.
- Refuse fatalism: systems designed can be redesigned.
- Begin the blueprint: rebuild constitutional function from the ground up.

Strategic Rationale

This chapter frames the stakes for the entire series. Before any solution can be credible, the scale of the problem must be named. Collapse is not theoretical—it is structural. By rooting the argument in the six constitutional promises, this chapter gives moral clarity and legal grounding to the restoration agenda that follows. It reminds the reader that these failures are not the fault of individuals alone, but of systems hijacked to serve power. This framing prepares the reader not just for outrage, but for action.

. . .

What You Can Do

Share this chapter with anyone who still believes this is politics as usual. Read it aloud with someone you trust. Talk about what you see happening—and what you're willing to do about it. Then keep going. The collapse is real. But so is the fight to rebuild.

Discussion Questions

1. What does it mean to form "a more perfect Union" when states are actively defying one another—and the federal government? Can unity exist without shared rules?
2. When law becomes selective, is it still law? What does equal justice require from courts, prosecutors, and the public—and how can we recognize its breakdown?
3. If chaos is used as a governing method, how do we distinguish crisis from strategy? What safeguards should exist to prevent the permanent normalization of emergency powers?
4. Should national defense include protection against internal sabotage and political manipulation of the military? What does true national security look like in a polarized democracy?
5. When policies increase dependence on the powerful rather than empowering the public, what becomes of the idea of general welfare? Who decides what the public deserves?
6. Can liberty survive when retaliation becomes routine? What is the difference between legal freedom and lived freedom—and how do we restore both?
7. Do you agree that the system is collapsing by design? Why or why not—and what evidence, personal or public, supports your view?

8. What would it look like to rebuild constitutional function from the ground up—not in theory, but in law, institutions, and practice?
9. At what point does the collapse of democratic norms become personal enough to act? What line must be crossed for you—or has it already been?

Reader's Guide: Chapter 2—The Broken Promises of Democracy

The Stakes

The Constitution is not just a slogan. It is a contract—one built on six promises: union, justice, tranquility, defense, welfare, and liberty. These were not vague aspirations. They were explicit goals by which the success of the republic could be measured. Today, all six stand broken—not worn by time, but shattered by choice. Democracy in the United States is no longer a system of self-rule. It is a stage—where the language of freedom cloaks the machinery of control. To recover a government worthy of its people, we must begin by naming what has been lost.

THE STRUCTURE

This chapter examines each of the Constitution's six stated goals, not as ideals but as operational criteria for a functioning republic. It traces each promise from its original intent through its modern violation—documenting how factionalism, retaliation, surveillance, and privatization have replaced unity, justice, and liberty. The structure is deliberately forensic: it does not plead for what might be. It reveals what already is—and how far the country has strayed from its founding obligations. Each broken promise is not an isolated tragedy. Together, they map a systemic collapse.

The Collapse

A more perfect union has become political warfare. Justice is meted by loyalty. Tranquility is enforced by fear. Defense has been reduced to spectacle, diplomacy to threats. The general welfare is hollowed by greed, and liberty has been rewritten as conditional privilege. These are not partisan failures. They are deliberate reassignments of government's purpose—from serving the people to securing control. A republic cannot endure when its founding promises are revoked. What we are witnessing is not decline. It is rupture—intentional, strategic, and ongoing.

The Remedy

Repair begins with restoration—reclaiming each constitutional promise as a measurable, enforceable standard. A restored union demands representation and deliberation. Justice requires insulation from political loyalty. Tranquility depends on legitimacy, not intimidation. Defense must be strategic and accountable. General welfare is not optional—it is foundational. And liberty must be uncoerced, unbought, and unmonitored. None of this can happen without political will. But it also cannot happen without public clarity. We must see clearly what has been lost to demand its return.

What Comes Next

This chapter is not the eulogy of a dying democracy. It is the indictment of those who broke it—and a reckoning with what will be required to rebuild. The road forward is not nostalgic. It is radical in the oldest sense: a return to root principles. Restoration is not revivalism. It is accountability. The Constitution's promises can still serve. But they will not enforce themselves. That task now belongs to the people. And the people must decide if the promises of democracy are worth keeping again.

Three Things to Remember

- The Constitution names six measurable promises—not just ideals.
- All six are now actively violated—not by decay, but by design.
- Restoration begins not with hope, but with the courage to name what is broken.

Action List

- Choose one constitutional promise and trace its local failure—then act.
- Share this chapter with someone who still believes the system is working.
- Organize a discussion or reading group to study constitutional obligations.
- Demand elected officials articulate how they will restore these six promises.
- Support lawsuits, legislation, and organizing efforts rooted in constitutional repair.

Strategic Rationale

Democracies do not collapse all at once. They are dismantled promise by promise, clause by clause, power by power. That dismantling can only be reversed with structural clarity and deliberate reform. This chapter defines the stakes: not just what we are losing, but what we must recover to govern ourselves again. It reframes patriotism—not as nostalgia for symbols, but as fidelity to the guarantees that make freedom real. Restoration is not theoretical. It is repair by design, equal to destruction by design.

What You Can Do

Speak the six promises aloud. Teach them. Post them. Live them. They are not rhetorical. They are the scorecard of the republic. Every reform, every vote, every protest should ask: are these promises being kept? If not, why? And what are you willing to do to keep them again?

Discussion Questions

1. The Constitution names six promises as the core duties of government. Which one do you believe is most foundational to the survival of democracy—and why?
2. If unity has been replaced by faction and coercion, what practical steps could restore national cohesion without silencing disagreement?
3. When the Department of Justice becomes a tool of reward and punishment, how can the rule of law be meaningfully restored?
4. How does surveillance-driven deterrence change the definition of domestic tranquility—and what boundaries should be drawn between safety and submission?
5. In what ways has national defense been transformed from protection of the people to preservation of power?

What consequences follow when alliances and deterrence collapse?
6. If the general welfare is no longer a shared commitment but a partisan battlefield, how can we reestablish it as a public good rather than a private opportunity?
7. What does it mean when liberty is conditional—available only to those who do not challenge authority? How does that shift affect the concept of rights?
8. This chapter presents the collapse as deliberate and strategic, not incidental. What evidence in your own community or state supports—or challenges—this claim?
9. Which broken promise most directly affects your life or community today? What would meaningful restoration look like in that area?
10. What prevents people from seeing this collapse clearly? How can that veil be lifted—through conversation, education, or example?

Reader's Guide: Chapter 3—Collapse to Country Again

The Stakes

America has entered a phase where democracy is no longer the default—collapse has already occurred, and what happens next will determine whether anything lasting remains. The six constitutional promises are no longer upheld, not by slow erosion, but by force. Yet this is not a postmortem. It is a call to recover. Collapse is not the end unless we let it harden into permanence. What stands between destruction and rebirth is not hope, but a plan. And what we do now will determine whether our children inherit a republic—or only its ruins.

· · ·

THE STRUCTURE

This chapter defines the five-phase strategic arc: Defense, Resistance, Restoration, Redemption, and Reinstitution. Each phase is tied to real power shifts and political conditions—beginning with Republican control and culminating in the deliberate re-limiting of extraordinary tools once reform is achieved. It escalates from delay, to obstruction, to reform, to legitimacy, to restraint. The structure insists on timing, sequence, and discipline. Each phase builds on the last and prepares the next. It is not theoretical. It is a survival and reconstruction strategy with dates, goals, and consequences.

THE COLLAPSE

Collapse is not abstract. It is happening now: courts ignored, laws unenforced, agencies hollowed, elections distorted, power seized without legitimacy. Every failure to act deepens the rupture. Every institutional silence reinforces lawlessness. The old message—wait, trust, endure—has become a weapon. Delay means surrender. The slow burn has become arson. And still, much of the public clings to the idea that the system will self-correct. It will not. No election, lawsuit, or protest alone can restore what's been broken. Collapse is not coming. It has come. But a plan can chart the way back.

THE REMEDY

We rebuild through five phases:

1. **Defense** (now): Delay authoritarian consolidation.
2. **Resistance** (2027): Expose, obstruct, prepare—with control of Congress.

3. **Restoration** (2029): Use the trifecta to reform law, courts, elections.
4. **Redemption** (2029+): Prove democracy can work again in daily life.
5. **Reinstitution**: Voluntarily return power to its proper limits.

This plan is not symbolic. It is strategic, moral, and time-bound. Without it, we drift. With it, we fight forward—lawfully, deliberately, and together.

What Comes Next

The path from collapse to country again is mapped—but not guaranteed. It requires leaders with moral courage, movements with real power, and a public willing to rise not just in outrage, but in action. The phases are not self-executing. If we do not build them, they will not arrive. And if we wait for one leader, one moment, one perfect plan, we will lose. What comes next is what we make. We know what is needed. We have the tools. Now we must decide whether to move—or surrender by standing still.

Three Things to Remember

- Collapse has already occurred—it is now a matter of consequence.
- Restoration requires sequence—Defense, Resistance, Redemption, Reinstitution.
- The republic's survival depends on execution, not mere opposition.

Action List

- Memorize and share the five-phase recovery plan.
- Embed it in campaigns, organizing, sermons, and local messaging.
- Build state-level capacity now for 2026 and 2028 wins.
- Identify and support leaders with reform courage—not just electability.
- Create infrastructure for community defense, truth-sharing, and public trust.

Strategic Rationale

The system has collapsed. Our task is not to mourn but to rebuild. The five-phase plan ensures we do not mistake symbolic victories for structural change. Defense delays collapse. Resistance exposes corruption. Restoration reforms the system. Redemption must prove the system earns its legitimacy. Reinstitution restrains power to preserve freedom. If we skip any step, we either fail or become what we sought to replace. Democracy must be restored with discipline—or it will not be restored at all.

What You Can Do

Share this plan. Study it. Teach it. Carry it into every room where power is discussed. Turn it into story, sermon, speech, and slogan. Do not wait for leaders. Become one. Build the next phase with those around you. Name what we are fighting for—not just what we oppose. Collapse ends when courage begins. And that courage must come from us.

. . .

Discussion Questions

1. This chapter argues that collapse is not a warning but a current reality. What signs in your own community or political system support—or contradict—that claim?
2. Why is sequencing so critical in the five-phase plan? What risks arise if we skip phases—or attempt them out of order?
3. Phase I defines delay as a moral use of time. How do we distinguish between strategic delay and passive inaction? What examples make this distinction clear?
4. Resistance is framed as obstruction with purpose. In what ways can refusal—tactical, legislative, or civic—serve democracy rather than hinder it?
5. The chapter warns that winning power without structural reform will lead to failure. What specific reforms must be prioritized during Restoration to avoid repeating past paralysis?
6. Redemption relies not on legislation, but on visible delivery and restored trust. What does successful Redemption look like in everyday life—and how can it be measured?
7. Reinstitution demands that we give back power voluntarily. How can we prevent reformed systems from becoming new instruments of abuse? What signs would signal it's time to step back?
8. Leadership is described as essential but not salvific. How can movements cultivate leaders who are both morally courageous and institutionally effective?
9. American Renewal is presented as a shared banner for action. How might you explain its core message to someone unfamiliar with politics but open to rebuilding trust in democracy?

10. The chapter ends with a challenge: if no one rises, we must. What role are you personally willing to play in this plan—and what would help you take the first step?

Reader's Guide: Phase I—Defense

The Stakes

Democracy has not ended—but it is under siege. The presidency is lawless, the courts are eroding, and Congress obeys the will of a regime, not the will of the people. There is no mandate—only seizure. In this context, the goal is not victory. It is survival. Survival long enough to resist. Resistance long enough to rebuild. Defense is the phase between collapse and resurgence. It is not passive. It is a strategy of interruption, exposure, and delay. And it begins with the truth: we have already lost power—but not yet the ability to disrupt what that power does.

THE STRUCTURE

This chapter maps a disciplined approach to democratic defense: (1) Hold the line through legal delay and judicial action; (2) Disrupt propaganda and expose corruption through independent media; (3) Mobilize civic networks to serve as an immune system; (4) Institutionalize habits of resistance—FiveFifteen, Immovable, community defense; (5) Prepare for personal and collective retaliation. Each paragraph builds upon the last, showing that defense is not disorganization but choreography: a sustained, many-handed refusal to concede what is not yet taken.

THE COLLAPSE

No institution has fallen entirely—but each has fractured. Trump's regime governs without majority support or legal constraint. Courts are threatened, mocked, and defied. The press is manipulated, bribed, and sued into silence. Congress cooperates out of cowardice, not consensus. And the people—many of them—feel disoriented and powerless. This is how collapse occurs: not all at once, but through paralysis and noise. Each time a ruling is ignored, a subpoena is dismissed, or a scandal vanishes beneath distraction, the foundation sinks deeper. Collapse is not an event. It is a process. And it is underway.

The Remedy

Interrupt. Delay. Disrupt. That is the remedy. File lawsuits not just to win but to expose. Demand press coverage that investigates, not flatters. Strengthen networks—legal, civic, journalistic—that resist intimidation. Establish resistance as a habit: five acts in fifteen days. Use organized hesitation—walkouts, refusals, slowdowns—as lawful disruption. Prepare for retaliation with personal readiness and community support. Above all: recognize that the regime thrives on speed and inevitability. Every pause you create—every gear you gum—gives democracy a chance to find its footing. Resistance begins where submission ends.

What Comes Next

If we hold the line—legally, civically, communally—we survive the phase of greatest danger. Then we turn to resistance, exposure, rebuilding. But none of that is possible without first enduring this moment. The point is not to feel powerful. The point is to become hard to defeat. Every document released, every protest mounted, every delay forced is a contribution to the next phase. What comes next depends on whether enough of us act now—not perfectly, but persistently. The next phase is not promised. It is earned. And this is how we earn it.

Three Things to Remember

- Defense is not passive—it is interruption by design.
- Institutions function only when people make them move.
- Delay buys the time democracy needs to reassemble.

Action List

- Commit to FiveFifteen: five acts in fifteen days—repeat.
- Support lawsuits, FOIA requests, and courtwatch programs.
- Subscribe to independent, investigative journalism.
- Build or join civic defense networks in your community.
- Prepare personally: legal, digital, and emergency readiness.

Strategic Rationale

Authoritarian regimes rely on inevitability, speed, and chaos. Delay fractures the illusion. Exposure pierces consent. Disruption forces recalibration. The longer we hold the line—through courts, press, and civil society—the more space we create for future action. This is not a final stand. It is a strategic one. If authoritarianism is a fire, defense is the firebreak. It slows the blaze. It preserves what can still be saved. And in that space, something else can grow.

. . .

What You Can Do

Pick your five. Choose your domain. Make it habit. Support the lawsuits. Fund the reporting. Join the watchdog groups. Protect your neighbors. Pressure your state reps. Learn what's happening—and then act on it. And above all: believe that defense matters. Because if we hold this line—just long enough—we get to fight forward. And if we fight forward, we win.

Discussion Questions

1. This chapter frames Defense not as retreat, but as deliberate interruption. What does that shift in framing change about how we think of civic action under authoritarian pressure?
2. Delay is described as both legal strategy and psychological defiance. Can you think of historical or contemporary examples where delay changed the trajectory of power?
3. The courts and press are still functioning—but under siege. What actions can ordinary citizens take to support their independence, credibility, and capacity?
4. How does the FiveFifteen model shift the idea of activism from sporadic protest to sustained habit? What would your five acts in fifteen days look like?
5. Movements like Immovable organize legal, nonviolent disruption. What forms of disruption do you consider both effective and ethically justified in a collapsing democracy?
6. Personal and community preparation is presented not as paranoia, but solidarity. How can we normalize readiness—without fueling fear or panic?

7. The chapter warns against chaos as distraction. What strategies help you stay focused on what matters, rather than reacting to engineered outrage?
8. State legislatures are described as the next battleground. What would it take for your state to become a line of defense—or a site of collapse?
9. This phase insists that the question is not whether we are powerful—but whether we are hard to defeat. What does it mean, in your context, to become "hard to defeat"?
10. What role are you personally willing to play in this phase —and what would help you begin?

Reader's Guide: Phase II—Resistance

The Stakes

If Trump's regime retains unchecked control through 2029, the republic will not recover. With the presidency captured, the courts compliant, and Congress inert, authoritarianism faces no internal resistance. The 2026 elections offer the only near-term chance to impose a brake. This is not about passing laws. It is about survival. Without a Democratic House and Senate, no investigation can proceed, no hearing can be held, and no voice inside government can still speak for the people.

THE STRUCTURE

This chapter lays out a three-part framework: expose, delay, and prepare. First, to reveal what has been hidden—from corruption to collaboration. Second, to slow the regime's advance using every procedural tool available. Third, to build the groundwork for the 2028 restoration, including the emergence of a courageous, unifying leader. Each paragraph aligns these tasks with a broader movement of defense, unity, and visible discipline—showing the public not just resistance, but responsibility.

The Collapse

Congress has not merely failed to check the executive—it has actively enabled it. Oversight was gutted, subpoenas ignored, agency corruption normalized. Judges rule without scrutiny, appointments are rushed through without review, and public trust has withered. The public's last institutional protection is vanishing. Trump did not need to dismantle Congress. He only needed it to surrender. And now, the collapse of legislative resistance threatens to finalize the authoritarian consolidation of power.

The Remedy

Retake Congress in 2026—not to govern, but to resist. Use committee hearings to expose suppressed truths. Legislate with purpose, even when vetoed, to show the public what is being denied. Delay executive actions by defunding implementation, mandating oversight, and slowing confirmations. Map corruption. Challenge captured judges. Force ethical reckonings. And above all, begin lifting a 2028 leader from the field—not from backroom deals. Resistance is not noise. It is strategy, visibility, and discipline.

What Comes Next

These years will not end in triumph. They are a holding action. But they are also a proving ground. In 2027 and 2028, we build toward power. Not just numerically—but morally, culturally, and electorally. The leader who rises must do so in full view—earned, not installed. The public must see resistance that speaks for them, that listens to them, and that builds trust through discipline. Every hearing, every delay, every act of courage is not just survival. It is the scaffold of what follows.

THREE THINGS TO **Remember**

- Resistance is not governance. It is exposure, delay, and preparation.
- Winning Congress is a beginning—not a solution.
- Discipline and visibility are the tools of democratic defense.

Action List

- Support campaigns in winnable 2026 House and Senate races.
- Promote public hearings and resistance legislation—even if vetoed.
- Share investigative coverage of corruption, ethics, and appointments.
- Attend town halls and demand visibility from elected officials.
- Track and elevate emerging 2028 leaders with courage and clarity.

Strategic Rationale

Authoritarianism advances by co-opting silence and disunity. By retaking Congress, we gain the power to disrupt—not end—the regime's momentum. Resistance legislation, vetoed bills, and exposed scandals shift public perception. Delay frustrates authoritarian consolidation. Unity prevents internal sabotage. We do not hold enough power to repair. But we can buy time—and time, in an autocracy, is rebellion. These are the tools of that rebellion.

What You Can Do

Win Congress in 2026. That is the front line. Organize locally. Fund strategically. Speak clearly. Track every veto. Amplify every hearing. Share what the regime rejects. Protect journalists, students, whistleblowers, and organizers. And above all—believe that resistance is more than defense. It is the evidence of a people not yet defeated. A people ready to govern again. If you don't know where to start, Appendix D has the tools. What matters is not scale. What matters is motion. Get in it.

Reader's Guide: Phase III—Restoration

The Stakes

Democracy cannot function on ceremony alone. For too long, the United States has sustained the appearance of a republic while hollowing out its foundation—turnout without representation, courts without neutrality, presidents without limits. The Restoration Agenda confronts this collapse directly. It insists that a democracy that does not count every vote, check every branch, and serve every person is not broken by accident. It has been broken on purpose—and must be rebuilt on principle.

The Structure

The chapter is organized around four categories: elections, presidential power, judicial legitimacy, and the civic trust. Within those, eighteen foundational reforms restore function to the institutions that make democracy possible. Each entry is not a policy proposal but an outcome demand—describing what must be true in a just and functional republic. They form a blueprint for repair. Later chapters explore them in depth, but here, the scaffolding is raised. This is the shift from protest to plan.

The Collapse

The failures addressed in this chapter are not theoretical—they are lived. Presidents govern without majorities. Senators block reforms while representing a fraction of the population. Judges legislate from the bench while accepting gifts from billionaires. Elections are manipulated, watchdogs are purged, and public truth is drowned by disinformation. The republic has been redesigned to privilege the powerful. These reforms do not assume dysfunction—they respond to it. The collapse is deliberate. The restoration must be as well.

The Remedy

Each reform makes democracy work as promised. Campaign finance reform restores public voice. Term limits for justices restore judicial trust. Pardon transparency and oversight enforcement make power accountable. None of these changes require rewriting the Constitution. They require enforcing it. The reforms are legal, practical, and necessary. Together, they form the architecture of a republic that governs with integrity—and answers to the people, not just the powerful.

What Comes Next

Restoration is not the end goal. It is the beginning of a government worthy of trust. This agenda creates the conditions under which deeper reforms—those rooted in fairness, care, and dignity—can take hold. We cannot renew what we have not yet repaired. These are the minimum conditions of self-government. Without them, no further reform can endure. With them, redemption becomes not just possible—but inevitable.

Three Things to **Remember**

- Rituals without fairness are not democracy.
- Eighteen reforms define the structural minimums for self-government.
- Restoration is not revolution. It is repair—of what was broken on purpose.

Action List

- Share the Restoration Agenda with local organizers or elected officials.
- Choose one reform and learn its local impact in your state or district.
- Attend or host a civic education event on structural democracy reforms.
- Push for legislative action or ballot measures on one high-priority reform.
- Track progress publicly—become a steward of restoration in your community.

Strategic Rationale

These reforms reclaim trust by fixing structure. Because the system was rigged through rules—electoral, procedural, institutional—those rules must now be rewritten. This is not a partisan plan. It is a democratic foundation. Structurally neutral reforms—

like term limits, funding transparency, and FOIA modernization—command broad support and unify diverse coalitions. That unification is the first step toward democratic renewal. Before we can inspire the future, we must repair the frame.

What You Can Do

Begin the work now. Read the reforms. Share them. Speak them. Challenge elected leaders to name them and commit to them. These are the scaffolds of a functioning republic. If we wait until power is won, it will already be too late. Rebuilding takes time. Rebuilding takes unity. And rebuilding starts with knowledge turned into action. Be part of that. Start now.

———✦———

Reader's Guide: Phase IV—Redemption

The Stakes

We cannot restore democracy if the end goal is only to return to what once was. Phase IV declares that mere survival is not enough. The Redemption Agenda offers a bolder standard: that a functioning democracy must do more than protect liberty—it must provide care, ensure dignity, and make justice real in people's lives. Without these outcomes, government remains abstract and unequal. The chapter marks a pivot from reconstitution to renewal, insisting that a republic worthy of trust must nourish the people who sustain it.

The Structure

This chapter is built on four pillars: care, education, justice, and belonging. Each includes foundational reforms that define what a democratic society must deliver to be legitimate. Eighteen core outcomes—universal health care, affordable housing, food security, labor dignity, criminal justice reform, and more—are not presented as a wish list but as minimums. These are not exhaustive policy blueprints. They are essential functions of a moral and competent state. The chapter culminates in a call to moral courage—not just policy ambition.

The Collapse

Every policy listed here responds to a national failure. The market has not provided housing. The courts have not protected labor. Our children grow up hungry, our infrastructure crumbles, our leaders trade sovereignty for profit. The breakdown is not hypothetical—it is the daily experience of millions. These failures are systemic, not accidental. Without intervention, they will deepen. The chapter exposes how exclusion, deregulation, and austerity hollowed out the promise of democracy and left cruelty in its place.

The Remedy

The Redemption Agenda defines what a democratic society must make true. Each reform is an outcome that cannot be left to market whim or partisan delay. The agenda emphasizes implementation over ideology: it does not prescribe one path, but demands a destination. A livable wage. Safe water. Trusted justice. These are the nonnegotiables of a democratic society. The policies may differ across states or parties, but the results must not. This is the moral floor of governance—not its ceiling.

What Comes Next

This is not where the work ends. It is where it begins to matter.

The chapter challenges readers to stop framing politics as a battle of ideas and start treating it as a test of care. Redemption does not come from Congress alone. It comes from the thousands of actions taken to ensure that someone eats, learns, heals, or belongs who otherwise would not. Readers are called to action—not by ideology, but by what is owed to one another in a democratic life.

THREE THINGS TO **Remember**

- Restoration makes democracy possible. Redemption makes it worth having.
- Eighteen reforms define the moral floor of a functioning republic.
- This is not a policy debate. It is a question of human dignity.

Action List

- Share the Redemption Agenda with someone unfamiliar with it.
- Choose one reform and connect with a local group fighting for it.
- Host or attend a discussion about care, dignity, or fairness in democracy.
- Frame political conversations around outcomes, not party loyalty.
- Ask every candidate: what will you make true for the people you serve?

Strategic Rationale

This chapter reclaims the language of government as service, not slogan. In doing so, it expands the appeal of reform beyond partisanship. The agenda is morally grounded but structurally universal: anyone—regardless of ideology—can fight for clean water, safe housing, or debt-free education. That cross-cutting appeal is a strategic asset. It creates a coalition of care that unites around outcome, not affiliation. It also reframes political ambition not as idealism, but as minimum decency in a functioning republic.

What You Can Do

Pick one item from the Redemption Agenda. Learn it. Defend it. Fund it. Talk about it. Organize around it. The fastest way to move the whole vision forward is to push one part of it until it changes a life.

Reader's Guide: Reinstitution—The Final Test of Democracy

The Stakes

This is the final chance to prove that democracy can outlive collapse—not through retaliation, but through restraint. Reinstitution is not a moment of dominance but of discipline: when those who saved the republic must choose to give back what was seized. If this phase fails, everything regained will appear as conquest, not correction. The world is watching to see whether American democracy can not only rebuild—but mature.

The Structure

This chapter opens with a declaration: that survival is not enough. It then explores how power, even when won justly, must be relinquished deliberately. Through constitutional reforms, sunsetting emergency powers, rebuilding trust, and codifying democratic norms, the chapter outlines what it takes to make democracy durable. It ends not with fanfare, but with a quiet handoff—the republic restored, not ruled.

THE COLLAPSE

Project 2025 and Trump's second term revealed how easily democracy can be dismantled by those who face no consequence. Institutions once meant to defend liberty were converted into tools of personal power. Checks were erased. Memory was manipulated. The emergency powers used to rescue the republic became dangerously indistinguishable from those that had imperiled it. Without restraint, even righteous reform can repeat the very abuses it sought to end.

THE REMEDY

We must now:

- Sunset all emergency powers through law, with oversight and expiration triggers.
- Make select reforms permanent through constitutional amendment.
- Restore balance to the judiciary and the executive—but then codify limits.
- Institutionalize trust as infrastructure: transparent budgeting, data, and oversight.
- Embed new ethical, redistricting, and appointment norms into statute.

Rebuild civic memory through education, museums, and public ritual.

This is the final construction phase—not a rollback, but a lock-in of democratic permanence.

What Comes Next

Reinstitution is not the end. It is the handoff. If we succeed, future generations will inherit a system that no longer relies on crisis for correction. They will grow up governed by fairness, not spectacle; by legitimacy, not legacy. This is the foundation for Volume III's final goal: a democracy strong enough to be ordinary—no longer an emergency, no longer a question.

Three Things to Remember

- Reinstitution is not revenge. It is restraint, written into law.
- What we give back now determines whether democracy endures.
- The final test of power is not how well it's wielded—but how freely it's relinquished.

Action List

- Pass laws and constitutional amendments that secure voting rights, judicial ethics, and term limits.
- Require congressional reauthorization for all emergency powers.
- Enforce transparency across budgeting, appointments, and service delivery.
- Rebuild public trust as measurable infrastructure.
- Anchor civic memory through education and culture.

- Finish reform—then codify fairness, even when it limits us.

Strategic Rationale

Without Reinstitution, every victory becomes vulnerable. This phase ensures that future leaders cannot exploit the tools built for rescue. It signals to allies and adversaries alike that democracy in America is not a fluke—but a form that knows how to recover and prevent relapse. By codifying restraint, we ensure that justice lasts longer than its moment. We make democracy sustainable, not performative.

WHAT YOU CAN DO

Track emergency powers in your state or nationally—demand they be sunset by law. Support constitutional amendments for ethical government, fair elections, and judicial accountability. Advocate for transparency tools—budget dashboards, open data, public access. Share stories and truth-telling efforts that preserve civic memory. Work with schools, museums, or local media to ensure this history is not erased. And above all, insist that the new norms apply to everyone—especially those you agree with. Democracy doesn't need defenders when it's convenient. It needs guardians when it would be easier to stay in power. Be one.

Reader's Guide: Chapter 9—The Responsibility of Power

The Stakes

This chapter is not the next phase—it is the final transfer. Once laws are passed and systems repaired, power returns to us. "The

Responsibility of Power" reframes the challenge ahead: how to wield the same tools that nearly destroyed democracy, not for dominance but for deliverance. If emergency powers are necessary to defend the republic, they must also be relinquished once that defense is secure. Without this transition, we risk becoming what we resisted. The chapter asks: Can we govern with strength and still surrender power?

The Structure

This chapter completes the arc of Volume I. It moves from collapse and response to stewardship and restraint. It opens by reminding us that Trump was not the cause of our failure, but the revealer of it. Then it recounts how power was seized—not through revolution, but through absence, decay, and capture. It shows how emergency authority, misused, became a weapon—and how it could instead become a shield. It closes by affirming that only collective, ethical, civic labor—not saviors—can preserve what was rebuilt.

The Collapse

Our failure was not just in permitting Trump's rise, but in tolerating a system hollowed out long before him. Courts were corrupted, agencies co-opted, Congress neutered, and oversight dismissed. Emergency power was not invented—it was inherited, dormant, and then abused. Every layer of democratic infrastructure became susceptible because it had been weakened by decades of disrepair. In the end, power changed hands not through coup, but through permission. This is the anatomy of collapse: when power is no longer accountable, and the people no longer sovereign.

The Remedy

Restoration is not revenge—it is repair with integrity. The same powers Trump exploited must now be used to restore justice, expand equity, and secure truth. But only for a time. We must codify limits, enforce oversight, and build systems that expire unless reauthorized under transparent conditions. The tools of crisis cannot become permanent governance. We must rebuild a government strong enough to serve, humble enough to step back, and trusted enough to endure.

What Comes Next

This is where the plan meets people. Every law restored, every protection reestablished, must be carried by those who believe in them enough to act. Citizens, judges, scientists, legislators, teachers, bureaucrats—this chapter is a call to all. The emergency will end only if we end it. The republic will stand only if we carry it. No election, no institution, no figurehead will do it alone. Democracy's survival now hinges on what we are willing to do—not once, but always.

Three Things to Remember

- Trump revealed, not caused, the democratic collapse.
- Emergency powers must be reclaimed, then relinquished.
- Only ordinary citizens, acting with integrity, can sustain democracy.

Action List

- Audit and reframe emergency powers to ensure for time-limited use.

- Demand full transparency in Supreme Court ethics and recusal.
- Hold elected officials accountable not just for votes, but values.
- Support local journalism, legal defense funds, and education in civic history.
- Encourage a civic culture of service—beyond elections and ideology.
- Elevate integrity as a civic virtue across sectors and professions.
- Push for statutory deadlines that force periodic review of powers.

Strategic Rationale

Democracy will not fail because its laws were flawed. It will fail if those laws are never lived. This chapter insists that self-government is not self-sustaining—it is labor-intensive and morally demanding. Trump's abuse of power proves that tools matter, but intent matters more. Strategy now demands a dual mission: to use the power we've reclaimed to rebuild what was lost, and to surrender that power before it corrupts us in turn. The fate of the republic lies in knowing when to stop.

WHAT YOU CAN DO

Refuse despair. Act with purpose—not with panic or passivity. Uphold integrity where you stand—whether in courtrooms, classrooms, city councils, or quiet moments of truth. Challenge those who bend power to privilege. Defend those who serve with decency. Learn your rights. Teach them. Share your voice. Fund what matters. Protect those at risk. Remember the past not as a warning alone, but as a summons. You are the republic's future—not a bystander, but a bearer of its promise. Live as if it depends on you. Because it does.

THESE READER'S Guides are not appendices. They are blueprints in miniature—meant to carry the argument from the page into the world. Each guide distills urgency into structure, and structure into motion. Together, they form a civic toolkit for those who refuse to meet collapse with silence. In classrooms, organizing circles, public libraries, and town halls, these guides can serve as catalysts: not to convince the indifferent, but to equip the willing.

Democracy does not require perfection. But it demands participation—ongoing, informed, and brave. These guides do not ask you to memorize arguments. They ask you to act on them. To teach, to question, to defend, to build. If the chapters of *American Renewal* are the frame, the Reader's Guides are the scaffolding—meant to lift the conversation until others can join. This is how we move from clarity to consequence. From knowledge to renewal. And from a republic in peril to one rebuilt by those who refused to let it die.

AFTERWORD: BEGIN HERE—THE REPUBLIC WILL NOT RESTORE ITSELF

———◆———

"History does not remember those who waited. It remembers those who began." — JP Vincent

You've now seen what we believe must be done—*American Renewal: A Manifesto for Resistance, a Blueprint for Restoration, and a Vision for Redemption.* You've seen the crisis we face, the window we have, the structural repairs required, and the deeper civic renewal that must follow. You've seen how far the promises of the Constitution have been allowed to erode. And perhaps you've disagreed with parts of it. That's good. Democracy does not require agreement. It requires urgency. If this plan provokes thought, invites dissent, or inspires better versions—then it has already done its work. Because the one response we cannot afford is waiting.

Democracy is not self-restoring. The Constitution was never designed to save us from lawless leaders or a captured court. It was written in the belief that we, the people, would do that work—that we would act before collapse, speak before silence, repair before rot.

Restoration is not nostalgia. It is moral clarity. It is the refusal to pretend that a sabotaged republic will mend itself.

We do not know what happens next. But we know where it begins: with you, with us, with all who still believe that power must be earned and law must be real. This is not a perfect plan. It was never meant to be. But it is a place to begin—before the window closes, before the silence hardens, before legitimacy is lost for good.

The republic can still be saved. Begin here.

— Jim Vincent, May 2025

COLOPHON

American Renewal is the first volume in an ongoing body of work focused on democratic restoration, resistance to authoritarianism, and the policies and principles that must define a just republic. Future volumes will expand on the thirty-six reforms introduced in this volume.

ALSO BY JIM VINCENT

American Renewal

Volume I of *The American Renewal Trilogy*

A manifesto for resistance, a blueprint for survival, and a plan to outlast authoritarian rule. Written to confront the second Trump presidency with truth, clarity, and strategic resolve.

American Restoration

Volume II of The American Renewal Trilogy

A comprehensive plan to rebuild the foundations of American democracy. Eighteen reforms necessary for rebuilding the foundations of democracy.

American Redemption *(forthcoming)*

Volume III of *The American Renewal Trilogy*

Eighteen legislative reforms to fulfill the constitutional promises—justice, peace, defense, prosperity, liberty, and unity—and build a republic that serves all its people.

Essays on Tyranny

A collection of essays on the collapse of American political norms between 2000 and 2024, and the cultural, moral, and institutional choices that made authoritarianism possible.

The Quiet Habit of Giving

A book about love, loss, and repair. Based on the six emotional needs that sustain long relationships—Admiration, Belonging, Control, Freedom, Security, and Validation—and what happens when they are missing.

ABOUT THE AUTHOR

Jim Vincent is a U.S. citizen, born and raised in the United States, where he lived for fifty years. He now resides in Australia, with children and grandchildren still living in the country he calls home. His writing reflects both an unbreakable connection to the American experiment—and a deep concern for its survival.

As an American living overseas, Vincent brings a perspective shaped by two advantages: distance from the tribal divisions that dominate U.S. politics, and the lived experience of another functioning democracy. From that vantage point, he sees with greater clarity what has been lost in the United States—and what remains possible.

He is the founder of *Jim Vincent US*, an independent publication focused on resisting authoritarianism and rebuilding democratic power. His work is trusted for its clarity, strategy, and moral purpose. He writes not for applause, but for action—believing that the republic must be reclaimed, not remembered.

He can be reached at https://jimvincentus.substack.com/

www.ingramcontent.com/pod-product-compliance
Lightning Source LLC
Chambersburg PA
CBHW061208070526
44583CB00025B/3166